CYBERTECHNOLOGY™

• A SHADOWRUN SOURCEBOOK •

AF538519

FASA CORPORATION

TABLE OF CONTENTS

PROTOTYPE #23IV-5TY9U-3DZ
RIGHT ARM SIMULATOR

CYBERTECHNOLOGY™

Writing
Tom Dowd

Additional Writing
Carl Sargent

Development
Carl Sargent

With help from:
Diane Piron-Gelman
Michael Mulvihill

Editorial Staff
Editorial Director
Donna Ippolito
Managing Editor
Sharon Turner Mulvihill
Associate Editors
Diane Piron-Gelman
Rob Cruz

Production Staff
Art Director
Jim Nelson
Project Manager & Layout Guy
Steve Bryant
Additional Graphic Design & Visual Kibitzing
Mark Ernst
Cover Art
Tom Baxa
Cover Design
Steve Bryant & Jim Nelson
Illustration
Peter Bergting
Craig Gilmore
Mike Jackson
Dave MacKay
David Martin
Karl Waller & Jim Nelson

Playtesters
Vince Esposito, Mike Florentine, Paul Fottler, Chris Hussey, Stephen Kenson, David Kingsley, Trent Lundsford, Mark Manhardt, Jeff Raven, Tarek Okail, Brian "Boris" Schoner, Darci Stratton, John Ward, Eric Williamson

SHADOWRUN® and MATRIX® are Registered Trademarks of FASA Corporation.
CYBERTECHNOLOGY™ is a Trademark of FASA Corporation.
Copyright © 1995 FASA Corporation. All Rights Reserved.
Printed in the U. S. A.
Published by: FASA Corporation
1100 W. Cermak Road • Suite B305 • Chicago, Il 60608
FASA Corporation can be reached on the GEnie computer network (E. Mail—FASA) on SCORPIA'S Roundtable (page 805) and on America OnLine (E. Mail— FASALou (Earthdawn), FASABryan (BattleTech) or FASAMike (Shadowrun and General Harassment) in the Online Gaming area (Keyword "Gaming")). Via InterNet use <AOL Account Name>@AOL.COM, but please, no list or server subscriptions. Thanks!

INTRODUCTION

Cybertechnology is a sourcebook about cyberware and related gear for use with the **Shadowrun** game. In addition to providing a selection of new cyberware, **Cybertechnology** re-examines the uses of more common pieces of cyberware present in the **Shadowrun** universe, doing for cyberware what **The Grimoire** did for magic and **Virtual Realities** did for the Matrix. **Cybertechnology** also introduces a new and fascinating (and frightening) concept to the **Shadowrun** universe: cybermancy, a unique blend of magic and cybertech that can keep characters alive long after they should be dead.

As with all expansion books, gamemasters and players may use any new rules that fit their games and discard those that do not. Gamemasters may also modify any of the rules in **Cybertechnology** to best suit their needs. However, gamemasters and players should agree on any new rules, rules modifications, and equipment before introducing them into their games. To make full use of the equipment and rules in **Cybertechnology**, players will need the **Shadowrun, Second Edition** (**SRII**) and **Shadowtech** sourcebooks. A few items in this book also refer to rules in the following **Shadowrun** books: **Street Samurai Catalog, Second Edition**; **Fields of Fire**; and **Shadowbeat**. However, the vast majority of material in **Cybertechnology** can be used without these books.

Cybertechnology is divided in two parts. **Part 1: Cyberware** deals with the familiar ground of cyberware in new and different ways. The first section of **Part 1**, **Life on the Wire**, is a fictional essay that discusses the ins and outs and repercussions of cyberware use. The second section, **Comfortably Numb**, offers brief descriptions of new cyberware, as well as discussing new uses and potential pitfalls of familiar cyberware. The third section, **Cyberware Rules**, includes optional, expanded and clarified cyberware rules.

Part 2: Cybermancy introduces cybermancy. It begins with the fictional essay **Beyond the Pale**, a firsthand account of experiencing cybermancy. Following **Beyond the Pale** is **Magic and Death**, a conversation about the ritual magic of cybermancy and the ominous hermetic mages who use this power to cheat death and reorder the basic processes of life. **Cybermancy Rules** offers rules and guidelines for incorporating cybermancy into **Shadowrun** games. The final section, **Chrome Kings**, contains a short selection of **Shadowrun** NPCs created using the **Cybertechnology** rules.

"I have taken all knowledge to be my province."
— Francis Bacon, 1592

The Shadowland BBS is temporarily unavailable while we update our interface to better serve your needs.

>>>>>(WHAT??!!!)<<<<<
—Bingo (09:33:09/11-14-56)

>>>>>(Geez, don't you look at any of the sysop posts when you log on? They announced this two weeks ago, and posted the message every day (in bigger and bigger letters—it was really cool).)<<<<<
—Raver (09:35:46/11-14-56)

>>>>>(OHMIGAWDOHMIGAWDOHMIGAWD ... I can't take this ... my persona's fading ... everything's going black ... Mommy?)<<<<<
—Bingo (09:38:23/11-14-56)

>>>>>(Drek—with such a gift for drama, this guy should be touring with the Enhanced Troupe of the Royal Shakespeare Company instead of wasting his precious skills on ten-nuyen runs and flaming his fellow deckers. NOT.)<<<<<
—Red Wraith (11:11:05/11-16-56)

>>>>>(Man. Even the BBS closing draws a crowd. You people need to get a virtual life.

You're getting the following post from Hatchetman courtesy of yours truly. Hey—I know all you netheads out there won't live long without your fix of the ol' Nexus action, so I'm givin' you what you need. Just do the usual thing to receive your very own copy of a doc that means a lot to me personally. And that's how I'll take any decking around with it, too—personally. Be polite, and we'll all live a lot more comfortably.)<<<<<
—Captain Chaos (12:54:23/11-17-56)

DOWNLOAD ALL? **OK**

NOTE FROM CONTROL—Anyone with any knowledge regarding sabotage to this system should contact me ASAP. Censorship will not be tolerated!

PART 1: CYBERWARE

WELCOME TO THE CUTTING EDGE

And I mean that literally and figuratively.

You've probably seen my handle clogging up these boards on several occasions as I gleefully joined in various gang-bashes and flame-fights here and there. I'm Hatchetman.

>>>>>(I told the boy he was wacked. Did he listen? Neh. Seems he was impressed by Matador's posting in the **Fields of Fire** compilation and decided to give it a try himself. "Sharing the wealth," as he said.

Personally, I think he's full of drek. You'll see bits of the truth in a few paragraphs if you're paying attention, but I'm going to lay it out for you. What follows is a purging of sorts, in my opinion. Hatchetman has found himself staring into the Abyss and I think he wants people to know how he got there. The following files are his confession, a sort of hypermedia last rites and search for absolution.

As I write this I don't know how it's all going to turn out, and I won't know for a few months. I thought about holding this section back until the matter was resolved, but instead I got Hatchetman to make me a promise. If he survived, I wanted him to tell us about what it was like—what he was like. All things considered, that seemed like it might be the most important thing he could say.

He agreed, and we shall see.)<<<<<

—Captain Chaos (04:20:18/11-17-56)

>>>>>(Shouldn't that be "last writes"? Heheheheheh.)<<<<<

—Warthog (20:51:14/11-18-56)

>>>>>(Crawl away and gack yourself, Warthog. Save me the trouble. Hatchetman's a friend, and this pains me a lot.)<<<<<

—Hangfire (02:18:10/11-19-56)

Okay, save the applause and the retching. See, I've been around. I'm not one of these whip-smart HyperGen tykes (as the media likes to call kids these days) who thinks attitude can substitute for brains and experience. I *was*, but I lived long enough to learn the error of my ways.

That may not be the case much longer.

See, chummers, I fragged up. Zigged when I should have zagged, trusted the wrong hombre, and took it on the chin (and pretty much everywhere else) with both barrels from a combat drone spitting armor-piercing explosive rounds from pair of linked miniguns.

>>>>>(Oooh, that smarts!)<<<<<

—Chuck-Chuck Razool (18:02:14/11-19-56)

I'm dictating this, so you'll have to excuse any lazy grammar. The doctors have a fancy name for the state I'm in that I can't remember real well and won't try to repeat. They usually utter it softly and gently.

The truth is, I'm pretty fragged up. I don't know how bad—I won't ask and won't let them tell me. All I know is, I'm dying—and I *would* die, if it weren't for what they're planning to do to save my hide. That's part of why I'm putting this posting together. When they're done with me, I won't be *me* anymore—but I will be alive and I'll be more than a brain in a box sitting on a table somewhere.

The corp I was running for when I got grated is one of the best in the biz when it comes to cyberware, and if you work for them beyond a certain level—do them favors—they're *very* loyal to you. That's why I'm still around. Though I got geeked (and that's the truth, 'cause I should be dead) the run played out well and they're feeling particularly appreciative. So I get to be the guinea pig. They're going to save my life by rebuilding my body.

>>>>>(There's only a couple of corps out there he could be talking about, but my money's running on Fuchi. Both the Villiers and Nakatomi factions are very hot on creating indentured cyber-servants. They rebuild you, but you owe them more than the literal pound of flesh.

I'm curious to see where he's going with this. If he's as "dead" as he's implying, simple cybersurgery isn't going to help him. I think they're talking about making a zombie out of him. If so, then he dictated this from one of Fuchi's gamma or delta clinics hidden away lord knows where. And that means someone slipped into the system and pulled this file without Fuchi's knowledge.

All in all, my virtual sombrero off to everyone concerned.)<<<<<

—Findler-man (19:14:31/11-22-56)

>>>>>(On behalf of several folks I won't name, thank you.)<<<<<

—Captain Chaos (21:32:44/11-22-56)

They've told me what they're going to do, but not too many folks around here can talk about it in simple terms and I can't deal with sentences longer than my rap sheet. There's another chummer around here, I'll call him "Priest," who they just finished fixing up. What they did to him is tinker-toy time compared to what they're going to do to me, but talking to him has helped. He seems to be okay, and I have no reason to think I won't be.

But back to the point of this whole thing. I've been around, and I know my share about being a samurai and about cyberware. I'm going to tell you what I know.

>>>>>(Oh gawd I've been hanging around for this??)<<<<<

—Trembler (00:28:13/11-24-56)

>>>>>(Pay attention—this is the proverbial Voice of Experience.)<<<<<

—Oswald III (10:55:20/11-29-56)

I'm going to tell you what I know about the ware out on the street, the stuff you rarely run into and the drek you'd better pray you never stumble across. I'm not going to tell you how it's made, how it interfaces with your nerves or any of that jetwash. I'm going to tell you how it *works*, what it *feels* like, and why you may or may not want it. And if you listen, you might not make the mistakes I've made.

LIFE ON THE WIRE

>>>>>(Hatchetman wrote this as an introduction to the nuts and bolts that follows. I kept this file read-only; I didn't want any of the usual drivel messing it up. Don't hack this file, children, or you'll answer to me.)<<<<<

—Captain Chaos (05:08:35/11-17-56)

I got my first piece of wire when I was thirteen years old. I'd lived all my life where I was born, in a torn-up section of Pullayup we called Fire Corner. It had a real name, but you can only find that on "official" documents and we didn't care about those. Fire Corner was our piece of the world, and if the rest of the city didn't give a drek about us, we didn't give a drek about them either.

Around my thirteenth birthday, my older half-brother Fizz and I were spending our time hanging with the local gang. We called ourselves—creatively enough—the Firemen, and our hangout—you guessed it—the Firehouse. Despite the name, we admitted chicas, too. We weren't completely stupid.

Fizz and I were just getting old enough (or smart enough—there were older kids than us in the Firemen at the time) to realize that nothing was happening with the gang. We weren't even really a gang; certainly, no one treated us like one. We were just the local kids who tended to stick up for each other. We called ourselves a gang because we figured that label made us Somebody.

Well, Fizz and I wanted to be Somebody for real. We'd barely started to weave all these asinine kids' plans into something interesting when the Slag Merchants came to Fire Corner. (I know, sounds like a bad tri-vid. But that's what happened.)

The Slag Merchants were a *real* gang of orks and humans who pushed BTLs, virtua-porn, and other lovely luxuries in sections of the Barrens north of us. For as far back as I could remember, a gang called Black Flag had owned Fire Corner, but we hardly ever saw them. (The same couldn't be said for local merchants and more notable street folk, but I was a kid. What

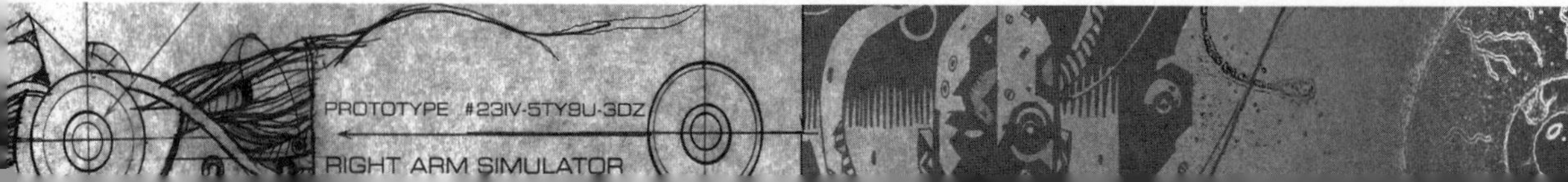

BERGTING

did I know?) We knew they pushed and pulled in our neighborhood, but we didn't think much of it. When we heard the Slag Merchants were sniffing around, that didn't mean much to us either.

Then one Tuesday night the little bar and food shack known as Leo's Den, a block down from the Firehouse, blew up. It happened early in the evening, which meant we were just hanging around. We rushed down to Leo's, right into a cloud of acrid smoke and a street full of flaming bits of storefront. In the middle of it, a tall, gaunt man in worn, tight black leathers, wearing silver spurs on his boots and a well-used pump shotgun on his back, lit a cigarette with a piece of the blown-out store. All the older folks and punks rubbernecking at the scene stayed far away from him.

He sneered at everyone and reached back. I thought he was going for the shotgun, but instead he untied his oily black ponytail. He ran the string through his hands and pulled it taut, like a garotte. Then he grinned and pointed at the store. "Not bad," he said. "Old wood burns nice. Keep that in mind."

He walked off, and no one stopped him. About halfway down the short street, he met half a dozen or so other leather-clad hardboys and girls, and they all jandered off together. Someone told me they were the Slag Merchants and that they'd taken over Fire Corner from Black Flag.

That would have been fine by us. The new owners had made their point with Leo's Den, and it was Leo's fault. He didn't want to pay protection money anymore—his mistake. Trouble was, someone else didn't want to pay either. But the Slag Merchants didn't blow up that place; a pawnshop made of concrete and brick would have taken a helluva bomb. Instead, they made their point with the owner's eleven-year-old son, Digger. They left him tied in various pieces to the pawnshop's security gate.

And Digger was a Fireman.

When our war was over, there were fewer of us and we'd changed. Fire Corner had become a place where we and ours died over three nights of mindless, childlike vengeance. To this day I wonder how it happened. Within a week of Digger's death there were less than a handful of Firemen left—but there were *no* Slag Merchants. None. We killed them all, women and men and one girl. We never learned her name.

I walked away. So did Fizz. So did Fizz's chica, Bethie. But all of us paid a price. Fizz lost three fingers from his left hand and gained a red scar down his back. Bethie had to wear her hair different to cover the burns at the base of her neck. I was blind. They told me I'd stood too close to the muzzle flash of a shotgun. I had to take their word for it, 'cause I didn't remember.

It was odd, how I felt about it. Ten of our friends were dead. Fizz and Bethie were scarred and I was blind. But none of that mattered. The Slag Merchants were gone and we'd done Digger right. If I was to be blind for that, so be it.

Fizz didn't see it that way. Two months later, he bought me eyes.

The damage to my eyes had been superficial, with little effect on the optic nerves. The street doc Fizz took me to, a tired gray woman named Ms. Chin (and not Asian, either) was pleased about that. She gave me two different models as replacements—the left a B&L Envisio 280L, the right a Fuchi-Tanner AVX. One blue, one brown. After three days Ms. Chin took the bandages off and installed the microbattery packs. I could see again.

My eyes weren't what I'd expected. All I knew about cybernetics, I'd learned from adverts and trid shows. The media's full of apocryphal tales about cyber-sams and street drek who decided life would be wizzer with wire, but it just ain't so. The people I know who got mods to stay cutting-edge were already in the biz. The people I used to know who got wire to get *in* the biz are all dead. I don't miss them.

On the trid, whenever they showed something from the slick cyber-sam's point of view they'd change how the image looked. I'd never really thought about what that would mean in real life. My eyes were like little trideo cameras. The image was too sharp sometimes, with too much detail. Colors looked different than I remembered. At first my left eye changed focus faster than my right, which gave me splitting headaches—I got that fixed after about a month. Occasional bursts of static or distortion cropped up without warning. I could see shapes better in near-darkness, but it was a lot harder to pick out details. The biggest changes were the most subtle. I could always feel them, especially in the morning when they felt colder than my meat body. When the rest of me felt wasted, the eyes continued to perform like machines. They also changed the way I saw.

I'm not talking physical vision—the cybereyes changed how I reacted to what I saw. They instantly distanced me from what I was seeing. For a while I felt like I was watching the world through trideo cameras; the eyes gave everything a sense of unreality, a detachment that made me a voyeur during the events of my own life. That level of detachment lasted only a few weeks or so after I got the focus problem fixed, but it made an impact. At the time, I welcomed it. I wanted to be apart from things.

The eyes were my first piece of cyber, but certainly not my last. I still have those eyes, but I don't use them. I keep them as mementos. One looks the same as it did all those years ago. The other is a little the worse for wear. I still have cybereyes—I never bothered with bio-replacements—but they're much nicer than the first pair—worth more than the average wage slave makes in a year. I can see in the dark, into the infrared spectrum, I see display data and such, and a bunch of other drek. Image quality is significantly better, mostly because of technological advances. The detachment is still there, but I'm used to it. Still, every now and then it creeps in, this sense of disassociation as I watch events unfold around me. I stare a lot, I'm told—unblinkingly because of the electro-static charge on the outer lenses that keeps the eyes clean. People say it's disquieting. I know what they mean.

I've used that detachment as a tool on a couple of occasions, when I didn't want to get emotionally involved. The people, including me, became actors in a trid-show. When I needed to, I delivered the ice-cold samurai's lines. I'd never have gotten through some situations otherwise. Am I proud? Not always. But I am alive and still in the biz.

Within a year of getting my eyes, I starting working as a runner for some yaks who ran book out of the back of a supermarket a few blocks from the Firehouse. The yaks had moved in when the Slag Merchants died. They could be more vicious than any, but they also felt loyal to the streets they worked. When a local nut named Thrace burned down the DeLosky tenement building it was the yaks, not the city government, who made sure the displaced people had a place to sleep.

After they found out what we'd done to the Slag Merchants, the yaks approached Fizz, Bethie, and me separately. Fizz said no thanks; they nodded and let him be. I became a runner for the yaks when I was fourteen, nearly fifteen. Not a shadowrunner—no one woulda known what a shadowrunner was back then—just a runner. I ran errands, delivered messages, did little things for the yaks. Over time, I did bigger things. They called me Cold Eyes.

I was sixteen when I got the spurs. Two of them, both in my right forearm. One extended past my wrist, the other in the opposite direction past my elbow. Ms. Chin told me she'd never heard of anyone mounting a pair that way. They made me dangerous, just like I wanted. Most people's spurs only go one way, to threaten the guy in front; the guy sneaking up behind isn't expecting to meet a blade in his gut from your elbow. I had an edge, and I used it. A pair of street drek tried to bounce me for the cash bag I was carrying, and I took them both down with a single swing of my right arm. It felt great.

My spurs gave me power. Even though I was just a runner, my spurs let me solve a couple of minor problems on my own initiative. The yaks kept an eye on me and liked what they saw. The spurs made me cocky, and it showed. I knew they were there. I could feel them whenever I twisted my right wrist. I lost a fair amount of flexibility in that wrist, but I thought the price was worth it. The spurs sliced some humility from me. I knew I could kill someone if I could reach them, and with practice I learned to make an attack look like a completely natural motion. I stood a little taller and talked a little sharper. On the street I took less drek and acted a little less afraid of the yaks. They took notice, and I moved up.

By the time I was twenty, I ran the runners. They all answered to me; I told them where to go and what to do. I also carried a gun by then, an old Colt Comanche complete with smartlink cyberware. That wire was caustic; I had to replace it twice before it worked right. By then I'd moved up from Ms. Chin to a bonafide yak doc. He wired the smartlink through my right arm, which made me wish I'd installed the spurs on my left. He also left a little scarring, but I didn't care about that much. Actually, I liked the scars. I thought they made me look like bad news. I was Somebody.

That smartlink interface made the Comanche feel warm when the safety was off. Neat trick, and it brought real meaning to the old adage, "Happiness is a warm gun."

By then, I took no drek from anyone I didn't think was important enough to sling drek my way. I alienated a lot of friends that way. I hardly ever saw Fire Corner anymore, and when I did few people cared to talk to me. Fizz usually did, though. He'd ended up as a bouncer at a local after-hours club called The Hat Rack. Bethie had OD'd on BTLs the year before, and Fizz had moved in with some joygirl named Mona. The only wire Fizz had was some razors. To me, he seemed small.

Despite my line of work, by my twentieth birthday I hadn't killed anyone yet. Not even the two slots after my cash bag; I'd settled for cutting them just bad enough to make them leave me alone. My first kill came, not because of any yak orders, but because I tried to help someone.

The yaks ran a meat club called Pick Up Sticks out of a converted bus terminal. It was a place where people of various sexual persuasions could drop by and pick up a partner or two for the night. It was also a meeting place for various underworld figures to shoot the breeze and strut a little. That's why I hung there. The club was upscale in a weird way—you know, that special kind of classy sleaze that slummers like. Performers of various orientations occasionally graced the stage in the back room, for the entertainment of the more hardcore clientele. In the main room were the wannabees and almost-theres and a lot of people who were just bored, tired, or in need of serious distraction.

I noticed the woman by accident, on what I suspect was her first visit. She wasn't the prettiest woman in the house, and not even to my taste. She looked part Asian, probably Japanese, and at the time my gotta-have ran to blond and stacked. I noticed her when she ran.

Apparently, she had second thoughts about whatever arrangements she'd been in the middle of making. I knew the slot she ducked out on as Meat Boy, a gleeful abuser of parasteroids and a club regular. He spit a Spanglish curse at her as she rushed away, her head bent in shame, then turned his attention to the other woman he'd been talking to. The one running away brushed me as she left.

I saw her again a few weeks later. This time she was dressed to fit in with the crowd, but still nervous. I noticed she drank more heavily. She left after a little while with a guy I barely glimpsed. She didn't show again for three weeks; then she turned up and this time left with a regular. After that, I started to watch for her. I wasn't sure why.

She showed a couple more times, the last with a stylish haircut a lot different from the corp-conservative look she'd been sporting. This time she hooked up with Meat Boy again. He didn't seem to recognize her, but she definitely knew who he was. I wondered if she was trying to prove something to herself. The two of them started to leave and on the way out picked up a short redhead that Meat Boy and I both knew as Nan.

After that I saw Meat Boy as usual, but not the woman—not at first. Then I realized she'd been turning up almost nightly for a week, sitting near the back bar with a clear view of Meat Boy's territory. She'd worn a red wig and was dressed down, acting like one of the many who came to watch the action. Mainly she watched Meat Boy, with an interest I would not have called either amorous or avaricious. She seemed to be working up the nerve for something.

About two and a half weeks after their little threesome, the woman jandered up to Meat Boy. At first he didn't recognize her in that cheap disguise, but when he jacked into it his whole attitude changed. He looked surprised, and then laughed at her. She flinched; he yanked the wig off her head and threw it away into the thrashing dance crowd. She said something, trying to face him down—I couldn't hear the words. He laughed again, pulled the low neckline of her dress out an inch or two and poured his drink down her body. She backed away. He said something else and made the universal sign for money—rubbing his thumb to his first two fingers. She stumbled away into the crowd. I didn't see where she went, and I knew confronting Meat Boy wouldn't get me anywhere. He was too big to deal with in any civil way, and I had no real reason to push him around. His final gesture bothered me, though.

I tracked her down through the credstick she'd used to pay her bar bill that last night. The info had been automatically logged into the club's computers. You'd be unpleasantly surprised to find out how much the yak knows and can keep track of based on simple transactions like that.

By cross-checking her name and other information, I found out exactly who she was and what she did. She was a staff lawyer for Renraku—not just any lawyer, but the head of one of their powerful Contract Task Forces. I recalled her prior behavior at the club, put it together with the atmosphere in those Japanese megacorps, and things began to fall into place. If Meat Boy had figured out what position she held, he might have tried to pull off just about anything.

I thought about confronting Meat Boy, but god knew what that could provoke. I thought about telling the club boss, a tanned weasel named Suko. If Meat Boy was putting the squeeze on this woman, Suko might take steps. The yaks didn't encourage that kind of "business practice" in the Pick Up Sticks. So I decided I'd solve the problem myself. Maybe I was getting uppity or bucking for a better position by proving my worth, or maybe I simply wanted the woman or was even pulling a primal "man-must-protect-woman" thing. Or maybe I just didn't like Meat Boy. I don't know. I had a friend pull together as much information on the woman as he could get without shaking too many trees. Then I made my plan to contact her.

My chummer had found out that she usually had lunch in one of the parks in the Arcology. I had an in with someone on the service staff there, so it was easy to get access to that low-security area and wait. She didn't show the first couple of days, and I started thinking about risking a cryptic message. On the third day she turned up. She sat down on one of the benches and began to nibble something from a container while working on her computer pad. I looked pretty casual myself and figured I could get away with simply approaching her. So I did.

I sat down at the edge of the bench, turned half toward her, and kept my body language and facial expression broad, open, and inviting to put her at ease and convince any Renraku guards or counter-espionage men that I was out cruising for a little lunchtime action. I told her I knew who she was, and I knew Meat Boy was pulling some sort of scam on her. I told her such activity wasn't appreciated, and that I could help her. Before she could reply or finish biting down on the carrot stick she was eating, I told her to meet me in the early evening at the Pick Up Sticks before Meat Boy showed up. Then I stood up and walked away.

By all rights, she should have called for a guard and had me shot right then and there. Just walking up to her like that remains among the stupidest things I've ever done. Amazingly, it worked. Two nights later, way before Meat Boy or any of the regulars showed up, she did.

She was scared, even more than the last time she'd talked to Meat Boy. I told her I worked for certain people who strove to maintain a certain reputation for the club and didn't appreciate Meat Boy's antics. She told me Meat Boy had set her up; he'd recorded his little tryst with her and Nan and was blackmailing her. In her position she was especially vulnerable to that kind of damage. Anything that might taint her integrity or discretion could prove professionally lethal.

I told the woman I'd take care of the problem, then paid Nan a visit. I knew exactly where she lived. Nan was easily intimidated. She gave Meat Boy up before I'd even finished my first sentance. Meat Boy had paid her for her part in the scam; apparently they'd pulled it before.

That night I watched Meat Boy at the club and waited until he picked up a pretty young thing. After borrowing a surveillance detector from Suko (while his back was turned), I dropped by Meat Boy's place about forty-five minutes after he and his friend for the evening got there.

I flicked on the lights at the most inopportune moment I could arrange and shoved my Comanche in Meat Boy's face while the girl ran screaming. Unfortunately, Meat Boy was as fast as he is big and stupid. He knocked the gun from my hand and the grin from my face while I was watching the girl. Too bad for Meat Boy I knew how to fight. He was so big and so fast that I had to kill him. I'd only meant to scare him and get the chip with the recording on it, but he didn't know that. He fought hard, and I killed him. It was messy; I managed not to think about it while I searched his place. The detector found the trid cameras in his bedroom, and from there it was easy to find the data drive he kept the images on. I knew enough about computers to look for parallel back-up drives, which I found and took. When Lone Star finally came by to investigate the smell, they'd find Meat Boy and the cameras and figure out what had happened. I knew they wouldn't care.

I met the woman again and showed her the hardware. She erased the files with her in them, and then watched impassively while I poured acid over the rest of it. And that was that.

Suko and the yaks, however, had learned of my activities. They were pleased I'd solved the problem, displeased that I'd done it without consulting them. There'd been some loyalty problems elsewhere in the organization about that time, and they decided they couldn't tolerate any insubordination. When all was said and done, I was out of the yak organization and visiting Ms. Chin again. Angry at the way I'd been treated, I refused to walk around with the yakuza brand of failure on my left hand, so I had the entire thing replaced. Nothing fancy, just a hand and some synthskin. Don't let anyone sell you paradise on synthskin, chummers, the drek is a *pain.* It may be slightly more durable than real skin, but it doesn't heal. When it gets scragged up, you gotta replace it. I've had to get enough new skin over the years to cover a thousand limbs. My line of work isn't kind to a body.

For most of the next month, I backed up Fizz a couple of nights a week and took odd jobs here and there. Then, out of the

blue, I got my first contact. Nothing fancy, just a message that some guy named Johnson wanted to meet me at some out-of-the-way location. The name told me this was more than just another odd job. I found out later that the contact and the run I went on were connected with Renraku. I figured I knew who dropped my name in somebody's ear, but I've never been able to prove it. I've done a lot of work for them since, though I'm no company man. Not at all. We just seem to fit well together. I've never really thought about why. They paid well, and through them I arranged for discounts on chrome. I was in the shadowrunning biz for good, and I needed the edge.

Eventually, my entire left arm became chrome. It also got banged up a lot more than the meat right. I guess I treated it less carefully. I knew it could take more punishment, except for the fragging skin, and so I kept sticking it where it didn't belong. I trashed it once, a surreal experience. I'd paid the extra nuyen for the full-function pain receptors (if the option comes your way *do it*; it will save your life), so despite the weight and motion differences the arm felt like it was mine. I scragged it tangling with a wendigo up in Athabasca. The beast and I were equally surprised when the arm came off in its claws. Pain dampers automatically cut in when something like that happens, so I felt a hellacious twinge and then—pop!—the wendigo staggered backward holding my arm. I stared at it. The beast stared at me and then tried to nosh on my limb. While it was tasting metal and getting more confused, I picked up my fallen Comanche and put two rounds in its right eye.

In time, I got a bunch of add-ons for the arm, but I kept it looking as normal as possible. Looking like two tons of death can be beneficial sometimes, but for me looking like a tough but still-human SOB was a better choice. Plenty of people suggested that I get the right arm done, too. Some docs believe things work better in pairs; I don't know if they meant physically or psychologically. I resisted—I figured one arm was enough. Looks like I don't have much choice now.

I got my first set of wired reflexes right after the wendigo incident. I hated them. They gave me a terrific edge, but I lost total control of my own body. With wired reflexes, you're *always* on edge. Any little noise, any little motion, could set me off. It took me years to train myself to handle the edginess. They're called wired *reflexes* for a reason. A reflex action is automatic; you react and the reflex takes over, removing the thinking/

judging/responding time from the equation. Perceived threat equals reaction, so you'd better hope the threat's real. Early on, I took steps to make sure I didn't lose control. As dangerous as it was, I kept my gun turned off. It took only fractions of a second to cybernetically bring it to a ready-state, and I needed those milliseconds to bring things under control.

I started doing all those things I'd spent years laughing at street sams for doing. I always sat with my back to a wall, not just so no one could sneak up on me, but also to force my *friends* to approach me from the front. That way, my wires wouldn't overreact and geek them. I kept my eyes open, watching everywhere, tracking the movement of everyone around me. I became paranoid by necessity. I was lucky—I never accidentally killed anyone. I punched my brother Fizz too many times to remember and sent more than one poor slob who stumbled too close spinning across the pavement, but that's all.

I picked up some headware communications gear along the way too and learned why street sams always seem to be talking to themselves. They're actually talking to Johnsons and fixers and contacts and anyone else that might give them a job. I found out that some of them talk to themselves to make everyone else think they're hot in the biz and tracking the scene. All too often, those guys are talking to their moms or calling the voice-sex line where their girlfriend works.

Bioware frightened me, and I resisted it for a long time. To me, chrome was chrome. It was machine, and I could deal with that. Parts of my body had been replaced by metal—null grief. Docs had been replacing parts of people with machine bits for years. Hearts, lungs, stomachs, livers, kidneys, and such—no one thought twice about it, and neither did I. But bioware, that drek is gengineered body parts grown to be better than the ones nature gave you. Also, cyberware tends to replace parts that don't work anymore (with the exception of some hardcore jokers, most of whom end up dead fast). With bioware, they go in and replace some part of you that's perfectly fine with a hunk of vat-born cells that do the same job and more (they hope).

So that drek spooked me. After a long while I opted for muscle augmentation, which I convinced myself wasn't all that different from cybernetic muscle replacement except in techno-babble ways that docs could argue over for hours. In the end, I was pleased with my choice. I could feel the difference—I could hit harder and faster, and handling really heavy guns or other gear wasn't anywhere near as much of a strain. I felt like I moved more smoothly, too, though I'm still not sure if that was real or just a psychological quirk. It felt like my whole body was more in sync with itself.

As with the metal, my first piece of bioware made the next ones easier to deal with. I had a street doc inject me with some symbiotes to get me on my feet faster after I'd screwed up and gotten hurt; they made me feel incredibly good, and I didn't mind having to carry around pocketfuls of stuffers. I'd always been a big eater and needed to exercise *a lot* to keep my weight down, so the symbiotes did me something of an extra favor. They also make me feel like I'm running a slight temperature, but I'm willing to put up with that minor discomfort. Funny thing, I haven't gotten a cold since I had the symbiotes put in.

My last piece of bioware was a nasty adrenal pump for emergencies. It's come damn close to giving me heart attacks twice, the most embarrassing of which hit me at an Urban Brawl game on which I had far too much money riding. They're not kidding when they tell you these things are touchy. My regular doc also tells me my blood pressure's slightly elevated, and warns me against salting my Stuffer Fries too much. Small price to pay, though, for a biogadget that's saved my life more than once. Because of that pump, I've taken hits that would have felled an elephant and kept on going long enough to get out of bad trouble. I paid for it with fragging-near-total physical collapse, of course; I'm talking a couple of solid days flat on my back, then another week feeling weaker than a baby. But I stayed alive, and that's the important thing.

I've gotten nothing much new in the past six years, except for minor parts and incremental upgrades to software and firmware. I had my bones laced with plastic four years ago, and I can feel that all the time. I'm not sure if the docs did a bad job or what, but sometimes I swear I can feel my joints grinding together. Then again, it might just be old age creeping on. Shoulda had someone look at it; a little late now, I guess.

So now I'm right on the cutting edge. Past it—or I will be before too long. They've described what they're going to do to me in terrible detail, and shown me pictures. I even got to choose how far they'd go. The simplest solution left me looking a lot like me, but that would have been a lie. The choice I opted for excited the docs. They actually *thanked me* for being "so brave." A real upper, that was. Sometimes I'm glad about it—or as glad as I can be, considering—because this way I won't die. I'm not ready to die yet. Other times, I wonder if this "life" I'm heading toward is really worth having. I never went to any church as a kid, but I know more than a few people who believe in something you might call a soul. If I have one, what's going to happen to it? Will it change? Will it just go away? Frag, will that make a difference?

I've seen them looking at diagrams and blueprints and then at me, as if they're visualizing the new parts I'll have. If I could still shiver, I would whenever they do that. Sometimes they laugh in disbelief at what they're going to do to me. It's impossible, and we all know it. I try to laugh too. It's not easy.

Priest told me there comes a point where the spirit decides that enough is enough and wants to move on. For this to happen, the body has to be either pretty fragged up (say, dead) or changed from the way it's supposed to be. Cyberware apparently changes the body that way; bioware doesn't as much, at least not for mundanes. Priest wasn't too clear about it. What they do around here, he said, is fool your spirit into thinking everything's okay and it should stay around. I told him that sounded cracked, but he just shrugged and told me they'd explained it to him that way. They use state-of-the-art biotechniques and magic—yeah, you read that right—to keep the person alive. They call it cybermancy, he said.

Cybermancy.

Maybe I should have thought twice about this.

COMFORTABLY NUMB

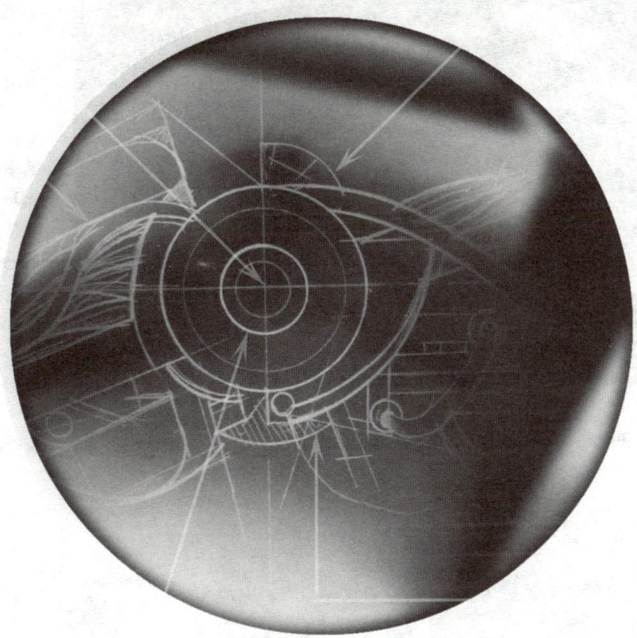

Plenty of stories about cyberware fly around the streets, lots of them tall tales and fake factoids. This file should set the record straight.

>>>>>(By his reckoning, at the very least.)<<<<<
—Findler-man (19:22:02/11-22-56)

I've had quite a few of the following pieces of cyberware myself, or I know someone who has. I'm telling you what I know based on my experiences or theirs. No ad hype. No medical techno-varnish. Just the chip truth, good and bad, chrome and rusty. Whatever I don't know or haven't run into, I expect some of the folks reading this to add (those of us who've survived more than a year or so on the streets just love to talk about all the neat tech we used to do it, doncha know).

>>>>>(Fraggin' aces, you bet. One man's scan is never enough for the Truth.)<<<<<
—Wonder One (02:29:18/11-27-56)

>>>>>(Why do I always get worried when posters capitalize Truth?)<<<<<
—Vambrace (21:07:56/11-28-56)

All opinions expressed are entirely mine, and sometimes even I can be misinformed or confused. If you make a life-affecting decision and things go horribly wrong, don't blame me. (If they go wondrously right and you turn a profit, and you feel obligated to me for my triple-A advice, that's another story. Donations accepted with thanks, assuming I'm still here to collect ...)

>>>>>(I'll bet he wishes he had chiploads of nuyen right about now. Then he could pay for the surgery himself instead of going in debt to a corp. I'd rather cack myself.)<<<<<
—Warthog (21:10:15/11-18-56)

>>>>>(I thought we'd already discussed this ...)<<<<<
—Hangfire (02:31:13/11-19-56)

COMMUNICATIONS GEAR

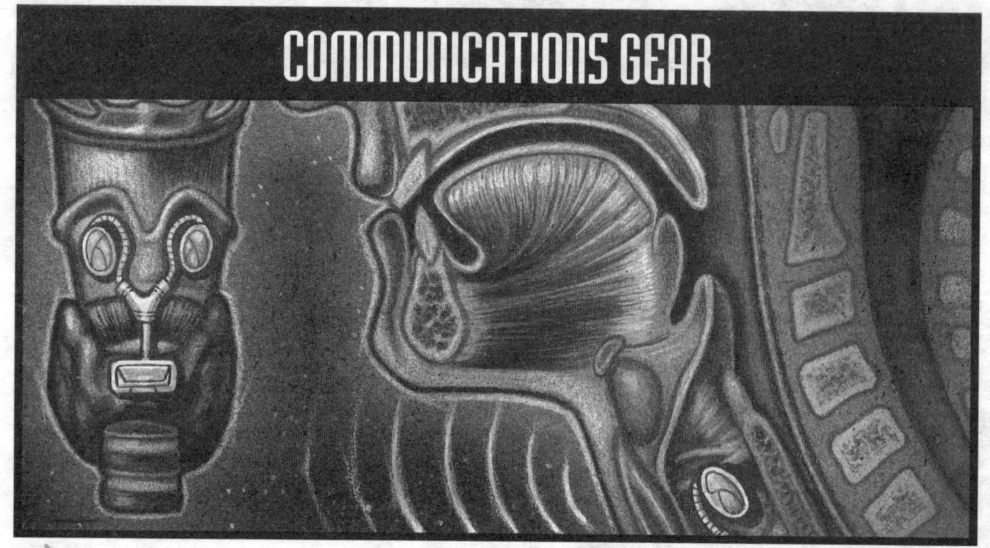

I've lost count of the runs I know of that got scragged up by botched communications. Get yourselves a decent headware comm setup: multi-channel, with signal compression/decompression for burst transmissions and hot-wire encryption/decryption to keep the corpers from listening in. A subvocal microphone and subdermal speakers are another must, if you want to keep J. Public from overhearing your nattering. Stay away from those fraggin' headset microphone combinations—any old joker can grab onto those and yank you around. Not too inconspicuous, either—a bad move in our line of work.

The best option is a pure cybernetic rig—a cybercomm link that works pretty much like telepathy.

	Essence Cost	Price	Availability	Street Index
Subvocal microphones				
External	—	500¥	3/48 hrs	1.25
Internal	.1	850¥	4/72 hrs	2
Subdermal speakers	.1	650¥	4/72 hrs	2
Cybercomm Link	.4	62,000¥	8/2 weeks	3

Subvocal Microphones

The external unit straps in place at the center of the throat. Either type of microphone adds a +4 modifier to the target number for Perception Tests made to overhear conversations using the system. Both units can connect to an external radio transceiver, the external unit via fiber-optic cable and the internal via a datajack (mandatory for such a hookup).

Subdermal Speakers

Usually mounted under the skin just behind the ear, these tiny speakers vibrate various bones in the ear to transmit sound. Sound coming over them cannot be overheard.

Cybercomm Link

The cybercomm link consists of a transducer and a radio transmitter. The transducer translates thoughts into words, so that the user need not speak aloud; the transmitter sends and receives these unspoken impulses. No external evidence of this system's use is visible or audible. Quadruples the number of spoken words allowed in a Free Action (p. 81, **SRII**).

>>>>>(Y'know what I hate? When you jump into somethin', and lo-and-fraggin'-behold, the opposition's on your frequency! If you've got crypto running hard then all you get is blasts of untranslated drek, but the multiple signals keep steppin' on each other and fraggin' it all up. I hate that.)<<<<<

—Jabber (20:24:18/11-25-56)

>>>>>(That's why you need point-to-point telecomm, bucko. Never fails.)<<<<<

—GrandPa (05:47:54/11-28-56)

>>>>>(As long as you have lineofsight.)<<<<<

—Hangfire (07:11:58/12-05-56)

>>>>>(Hey Jabber, how about changing channels when that happens? Just a thought.)<<<<<

—Weasel Boy (22:00:45/12-08-56)

CYBEREYES

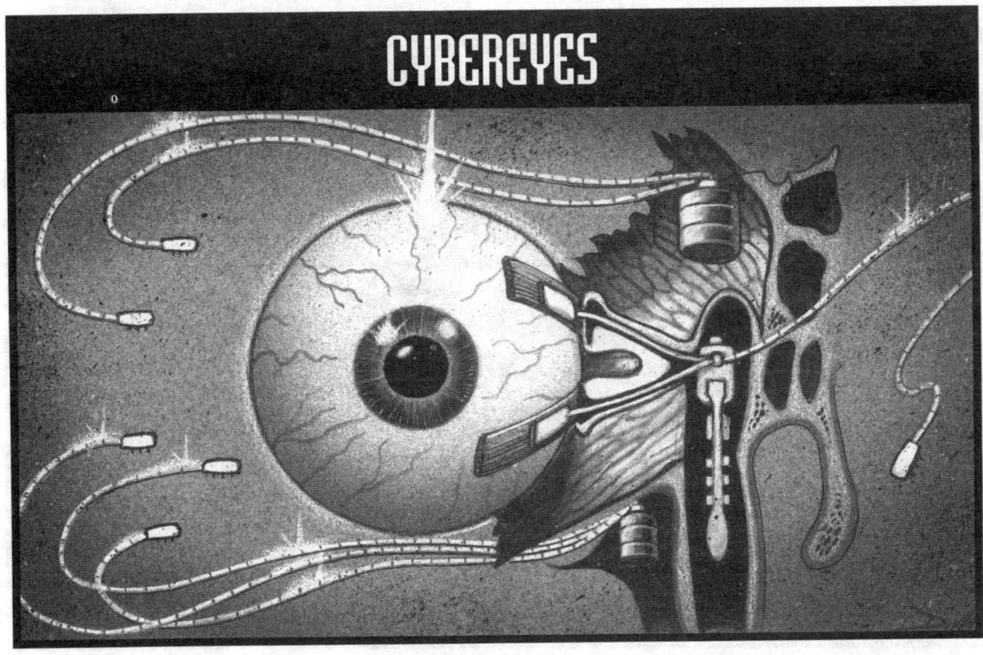

I've had cybereyes awhile, and so do more folks than you might think. The top sellers are made to look real, so they're tough to spot. A drek-load of new cybereye gear hits the market all the time, some of which is pretty handy. If you see two versions of something, go for the name brand or the more expensive piece; better to pay a little more for quality than go cheap and have it fail at the worst moment. When in doubt, ask around. Somebody somewhere probably uses it and can give you the clean scan.

Cybereyes come with cleaning kits; USE THEM!!! All the precautions in the fraggin' universe won't keep foreign drek out of the eye socket, and some of the parts are so delicate they can get really fragged up that way.

Wiz but trivial eye gadgets that I like include the retinal clock, the image link, and protective covers. Covers cut down the amount of drek I'll eventually have to deal with, meaning I don't need to clean the eyes as often (especially at inconvenient times!). The image link lets me patch in vidphone images, so I can see who I'm talking to right in my field of vision. As for the clock, I just like to know what time it is. I'm funny that way.

	Essence Cost	Price	Availability	Street Index
Retinal Clock	.1	450¥	3/24 hrs	1
Image Link	.2	1,600¥	4/48 hrs	2
Protective Covers	0	500¥	4/48 hrs	1.5

Retinal Clock

Displays a time/date stamp in the lower right corner of the wearer's field of vision or wherever the user wants. Can be modified for region and season and includes a stopwatch style timer and a countdown timer. Accurate to +/– .0001 seconds per year.

Image Link

Allows the display of a vidphone image within the field of vision and functions as a Display Link (p. 247, **SRII**).

Protective Covers

Protects cyber and normal eyes against impact and particles. Available in standard transparent or one-way reflective material; one-way adds 20 percent to the price. At the gamemaster's discretion, covers give 1 point of Impact Armor to the eye area.

>>>>>(Poetic tradition has long held that the eyes are windows to the soul. I can usually spot a chummer with cybereyes, no matter how natural they're supposed to look. It's not anything textural, like odd reflections or motion. They're just—cold.)<<<<<

—Earth Mother VI (12:18:45/11-29-56)

>>>>>(I wouldn't go that far, but I agree with Hatchetman's comments about feelings of detachment. Psychologists call it "disassociation syndrome," and it's treatable with emotion-support therapy. Check the telecom listings—half those jokers note it in their ads.)<<<<<

—Findler-man (02:54:48/12-02-56)

>>>>>(That's because they treat burned-out wageslaves with the same techniques.)<<<<<

—Social Adept (03:21:40/12-07-56)

EYE DATAJACKS

These wiz little toys deserve special mention. One type is an eye dataport, the other an optical scanning datajack. The dataport sits behind the iris of the cybereye. You reach up, apply a little pressure to the iris, and it opens to reveal a standard dataport. This toy is handy for sleazing your way into places that someone might try to keep you out of if you happened to be wearing a standard (and visible) datajack. It's tough to tell what's buried in a cybereye without dissecting the whole thing. Drawback is, you end up standing around with your eye plugged into something. Very weird—likely to attract attention if anyone happens along.

The optical scanning datajack includes an emitter unit and a data receptor. The receptor sits in your eye; the emitter you carry around (it's no bigger than a silver oxide battery). You stick the emitter unit onto the data-out port on whatever you came hunting for and you look at it. The data receptor in your eye reads the laser beam put out by the emitter and decodes the data transmitted over it. Dozens of uses for this, neh? It's cutting edge drek, but becoming more available.

	Essence Cost	**Cost**	**Availability**	**Street Index**
Eye Dataport	.25	2,200¥	6/48 hrs	2
Optical Scanning Datajack	.3	5,500¥	8/72 hrs	3

	Concealability	**Weight**	**Availability**	**Cost**	**Street Index**
Optical Scanning Datajack Emitter	10	.25	8/2 weeks	2,500¥	2

>>>>>(Wow, wiz stuff. Yeah, he's right. The implications for this optical scanning datajack are pretty hefty. How come we haven't heard about it before?)<<<<<

—Weasel Boy (03:21:18/12-02-56)

>>>>>(Perhaps surprisingly, Ares owns the international patents on this technology, and they've been keeping it to themselves. You can get it sometimes on the shadowmarket, but it takes awhile.)<<<<<

—Findler-man (20:19:41/12-03-56)

>>>>>(What kind of implications?)<<<<<

—Mooch (21:19:23/12-04-56)

>>>>>(Security, Mooch. Data couriers. Data manipulation. Data theft. Think about it.)<<<<<

—Findler-man (11:08:54/12-05-56)

EYE LIGHT SYSTEMS

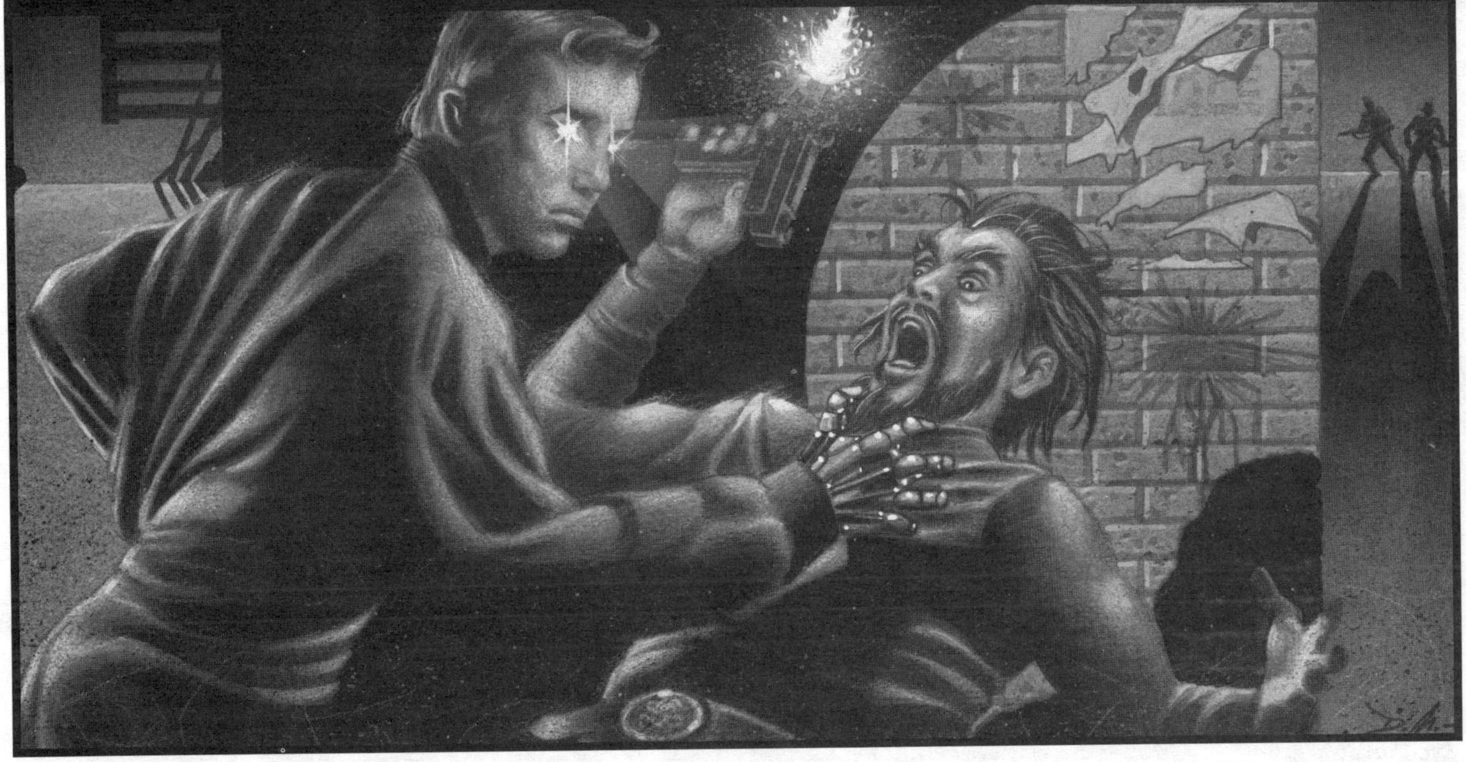

Eye lights, another nifty new piece of work, can be either a tool or a weapon. The plain-vanilla light system mounts high-powered, low-heat lights in the cybereye that channel a tight, polarized beam outward down a path parallel to the optical center of the eye. An amount of light sufficient to see with standard low-light eyes falls wherever the user is looking. The tight beam and polarization minimize scatter from the eye, so the light can't be seen unless someone's staring right at you.

You can also get a nasty, nasty high-intensity BrightLight flash system. Brights come in two intensities; the first is reusable and works just like a flash-pak. The second is a one-shot deal until the flash units are replaced; this puppy creates a flash bright enough to overload the optic nerves of the poor bastard in front of you, blinding and stunning him at the same time.

	Essence Cost	**Price**	**Availability**	**Street Index**
Eye Light Systems	.2	1,200¥	4/72 hrs	1.5
BrightLight Addition	.4	1,200¥	8/2 weeks	3
w/ Flash-pak	—	+1,000¥	8/2 weeks	3
each One Shot Flash-pak	—	+500¥	8/2 weeks	3

>>>>>(I've heard of lights so bright they hurt, but—whew!)<<<<<
—Erinzyle (12:54:32/11-23-56)

>>>>>(I wonder how long the fragger stays down?)<<<<<
—Dozer (13:22:43/11-23-56)

>>>>>(I wonder how come you don't blind yourself using these things.)<<<<<
—Ludwig (13:42:34/11-23-56)

>>>>>(The system compensates for the flash, drekbrain. Use your fraggin' head!)<<<<<
—Logik (13:55:33/11-23-56)

There are enough deranged minds in the world that *somebody* had to be working on these things. Eye weapons have specific and limited uses, and I don't recommend them in normal combat situations. For one thing, using them tends to leave you partially blind, at least for awhile. Firing a gun in your eye also inflicts quite a few shocks—like some nasty recoil, for example—but if you're willing to live with that, one of these things might just save your life.

The two types of eye weapons available are a dart and a gun, and they work in similar ways. One ammo load sits in the eye, and is fired through a hole running parallel to the optical axis. When the weapon fires, a sheer covering tears away and reveals the barrel. The eye dart fires Narcoject or toxin rounds; the eye gun fires microbullets. And yes, you can install these weird gadgets in more than one eye.

	Essence Cost	Price	Availability	Street Index
Eye Dart	.25	4,200¥	8/2 weeks	2
Eye Gun	.4	6,400¥	6/1 week	3

Eye Dart

Fires half-strength (round up) Narcoject/toxin rounds as a hold-out pistol with one-half range (round down). One shot per reload. Reloading takes 10 Combat Turns. Rounds cost four times the normal price. Firing requires a Special Skill or Quickness Test. Cannot be linked to any kind of aim enhancer. See p. 62, **Street Samurai Catalog**, for Narcoject weapons; p. 186, **SRII**, for toxins; and pp. 90, 92, 97, **Shadowtech**, for other compounds. After firing, a character must apply a +2 modifier to all visual tests for a period of (4 – Unaugmented Body) Combat Turns, for a minimum of 1 Combat Turn. For rules on the maximum capacity of the orbital socket, see **Cyberware Rules**, p. 45.

Eye Gun

Treat as a hold-out pistol with one-half range (round down), a –1 Damage modifier, and a +1 recoil modifier. One shot per reload. Reloading takes 10 Combat Turns, but a successful Biotech Test reduces the reload time by half the character's Quickness. Rounds cost five times the normal price. Firing requires a Special Skill or Quickness Test. Cannot be linked to any kind of aim enhancer. After firing, a character must apply a +2 modifier for all visual tests for a period of (6 – Unaugmented Body) Combat Turns, for a minimum of 2 Combat Turns.

>>>>>(These are the stupidest things I've ever seen. Their only merit is concealability, and most security-smart people have wised up to the eye weapon. You're far better off sticking a mini-weapon in your mouth; the oral cavity is a lot bigger than your eye socket, and you can pack a lot more inside it. Plus, you can only fit so much into a cybereye. Filling it with a poxy little weapon that might let you gun down a rat at three yards means foregoing a lot of more useful equipment. I've also heard some spectacularly unpleasant stories about damage to cybereye systems and the optic nerve from over-enthusiastic recoil. And don't even think about blocked gun barrels.

Friend of a friend got into a situation where you'd expect an eye gun to be helpful—captured for interrogation, scanned and searched, but the metallic mass of his cybereye obscured the weapon inside. Unfortunately for him, the interrogators knew all about eye guns and interrogated him from behind a bulletproof glass shield. When he played his final trump card, the bullet ricocheted and hit him in a place that makes him sing soprano these days. Serves him right, the stupid slag.

Someday, someone might manage to create a really effective eye gun, even with the obvious major constraints (the size of the bullet, for example). Until then, leave this kind of thing to wannabees and idiots.)<<<<<

—MesoStim (18:22:19/07-17-56)

EYE LASER SYSTEMS

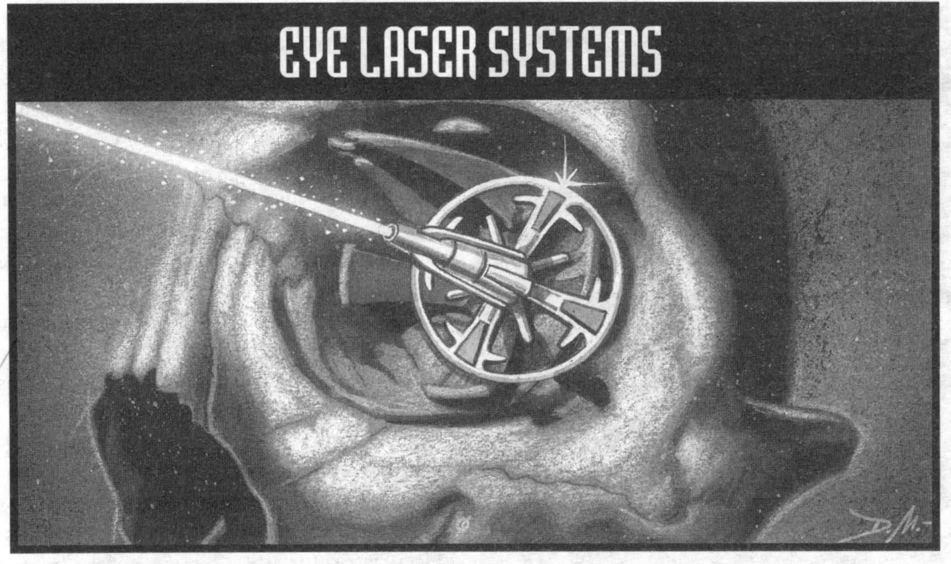

No combat lasers yet, chummers. Gotta wait a few more years for those. Wiz drek you *can* get includes laser designators, laser trackers, and tool lasers. Word of warning—if someone tries to sell you a headware laser sight and gun-link system, ignore it. Buy a smartgun system or a simple laser sight. Why bother with the cost and hassle of putting cyberdrek in your head when the tech you can carry around works better?

Laser designators do the targeting work for other weapons, just like the full-size units, but at slightly reduced ranges. I know some people who've put tracking weapon mounts on vehicles or drones and slaved them to their eye-laser designator frequencies. Interesting technique, but it implies a scale of combat I'd rather not think about. Me, I'm a hot-flash skirmish man. You won't find me at any tactical engagements.

Laser trackers are laser sights cybernetically tied to a cyberarm that automatically tracks with the sight. The arm tracks exactly where you're looking and aims. Very wiz. Tool lasers can create small welds and cut thin objects, but are too low-powered to cause more than minimal damage. They have their uses, but don't count on hurting somebody much with one.

	Range (in meters)	Essence Cost	Price	Availability	Street Index
Laser Designator	4,000	.5	12,000¥	12/1 month	3
Laser Tracker	400	.2	3,200¥	8/72 hrs	2
Tool Laser	4	.25	5,200¥	8/1 week	2

Laser Designator

See pp. 60 and 85, **Fields of Fire**, for more information on laser designators. Maximum range is 1,000 meters.

Laser Tracker

Ties into a cyberlimb or external weapon mount and auto-tracks a designated target. This function is built into the unit and does not require an additional laser designator.

Tool Laser

The tool laser has a Damage Code of 4L. If it is used as a weapon, make Combat Tests using the character's Quickness or a Special Skill. These tests have a Base Target Number 4, with a +1 modifier to the target number for each meter or part thereof beyond 1. The Power of the attack is –1 against targets up to two meters away and –2 against targets up to four meters away. Will not penetrate reflective metals or silvered glass, but can cut mirrored plastics.

>>>>>(I've used the tool laser more than once as a little surprise. If you're savvy enough and a little lucky, you can kill someone by burning the beam right into their eye or ear and deep into their skull.)<<<<<

—Skulker (14:08:54/12-01-56)

>>>>(All the more reason to wear those mirror-shades, neh?)<<<<<

—Weasel Boy (23:21:08/12-04-56)

>>>>>(Just make sure they're not plastic or cheap glass. Too many impurities or imperfections and it'll start to burn instead of reflecting the laser.)<<<<<

—Findler-man (04:27:50/12-05-56)

>>>>>(Um, wouldn't that stop the beam, too?)<<<<<

—Weasel Boy (22:41:32/12-06-56)

CYBEREAR ACCESSORIES

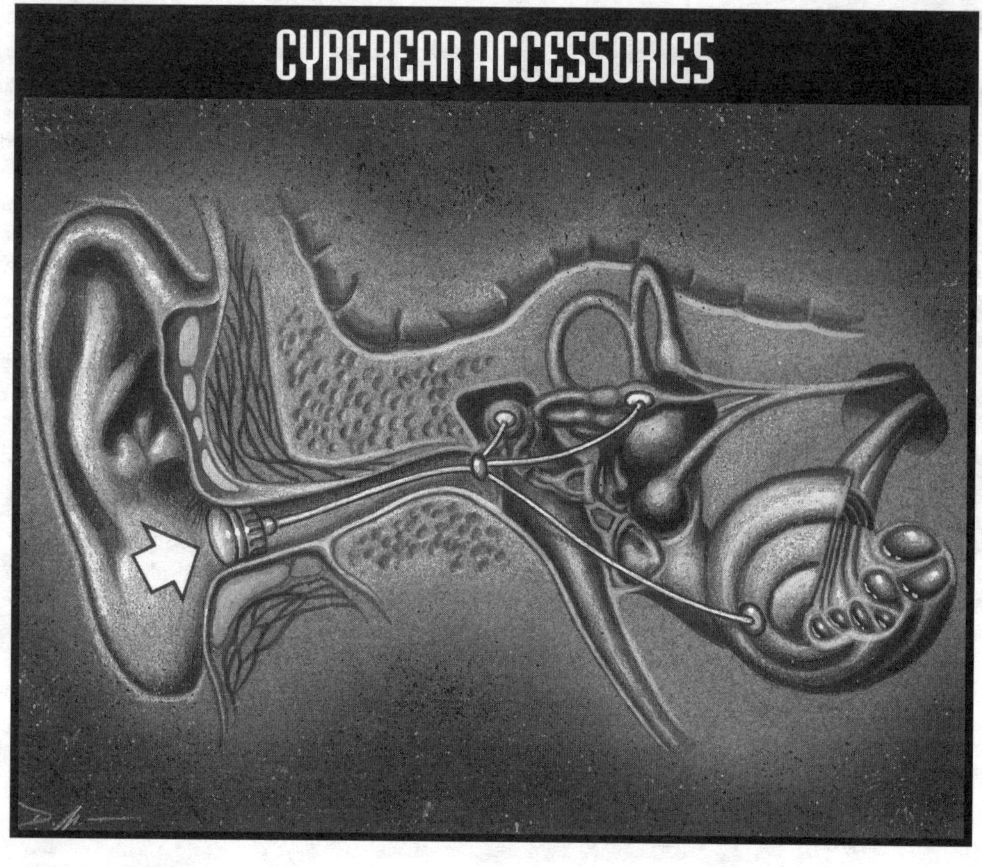

Compared to eyes, cyberears are simple. The market's pretty saturated with cyberear drek already, but I know of a couple of interesting toys. The first is a spatial recognizer, which improves on nature's ability to tell where a sound is coming from. This thing helps you locate the source of what you're hearing—always useful when you're trying to place how far behind you the pounding footsteps are, or the location of the sniper whose foot you just heard scraping against the side of a chimney. It's especially handy in situations where you might be fooled by echoes.

Another nifty cyberear gadget augments the inner ear's natural balance sensors. A friend of mine has one, and I've seen him do some pretty amazing things. He was pretty athletic even before he got the balance augmentor, but now he can jump around and swing from things and hardly ever fall down. He doesn't even wobble for a second, except under rare circumstances. My buddy also tells me the gadget makes it harder for him to deliberately fall down or throw himself off balance. He had to train himself to do that all over again. Weird.

	Essence Cost	Price	Availability	Street Index
Spatial Recognizer	.2	1,200¥	4/48 hrs	2
Balance Augmentor	.4	14,000¥	8/2 weeks	2

Spatial Recognizer

This cyberear accessory reduces the target numbers for Perception Tests based primarily on sound location by –2 whenever a character attempts to track something by listening for movement. For additional rules in cases of restricted vision, see **Cyberware Rules**, p. 46.

Balance Augmentor

This device reduces the target numbers by –2 for any Skill Tests involving balance, such as climbing, walking across a narrow platform, landing after a jump, and so on. It also applies a –2 modifier in the character's favor to avoid Knockdown (see pp. 91–92 and p. 103, **SRII**).

>>>>>(A buddy of mine has the cybereye light system and the spatial whatchamajigs. He is hellaciously dangerous in the dark. I've seen him take on half a dozen well-trained men in near-dark and kick ass. Their training told them to go on the defensive and TURN ON THE LIGHTS when fighting in the dark. They didn't do too well.)<<<<<

—Mugger Hugger (14:23:54/12-02-56)

>>>>>(I hear you should turn off the balance augmentor when you're trying to fly a plane or do anything that deliberately plays with your sense of balance. A friend of mine knows a guy who was wrecked for a week because he forgot to deactivate his augmentor before getting into a roller coaster.)<<<<<

—Weasel Boy (10:45:35/12-05-56)

>>>>>(I'll give you dangerous: attack dogs with the balance enhancer.)<<<<<

—Findler-man (01:32:08/12-06-56)

ORAL WEAPONS

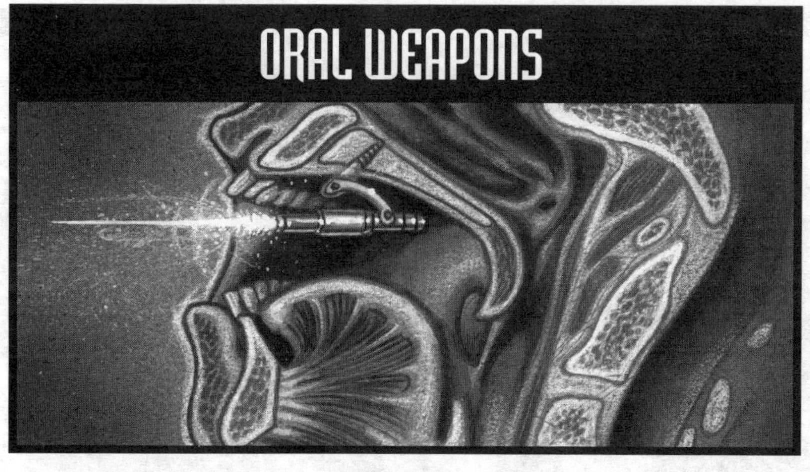

Never mind the obvious jokes—some of these actually work and might save your lousy hides someday. Oral darts, guns, spurs and whips may sound weirder than a cross between a hellhound and a toy poodle, but they have their uses. The oral dart and the oral gun work pretty much the same. Each one stores a few rounds of ammo in a cavity in the roof of the mouth, and each has a safety to keep them from firing unless the user's mouth is open. The dart fires mini-Narcoject or toxin rounds, the gun microbullets. As bizarre as these sound, the sheer surprise value may be worth it for some. I've never used either of them, but friends of mine have.

The spur and the whip I find so weird as to be useless, but others may disagree. The oral spur is misnamed, I think. Maybe the slots who make this thing couldn't stomach the thought of marketing an oral ram. The spur's pneumatic trigger uses your own lungs plus some pumps—just prime the system and WHAM. The whip also has a pneumatic, self-priming trigger—and no, you can't get a mono-whip version. Just imagine how much fun that would be to use, neh? Anyone for slicing off his own nose?

	Essence Cost	Price	Availability	Street Index
Oral Dart	.25	3,600¥	6/1 weeks	2
Oral Gun	.4	5,600¥	6/72 hrs	3
Oral Spur	.25	8,200¥	6/72 hrs	2.5
Oral Whip	.25	10,500¥	8/1 week	2.5

Oral Dart

Fires Narcoject/toxin rounds at hold-out pistol ranges. Can hold three darts before reloading, which takes 1 minute per dart. Ammo costs double the standard price. Use a Special Skill or Quickness for the Ranged Combat Test. Cannot be linked to aim enhancers.

Oral Gun

Treat as a hold-out pistol with a total of four shots. Reloading takes one minute per shot. Ammo costs triple the standard price. Use a Special Skill or Quickness for the Ranged Combat Test. Cannot be linked to aim enhancers.

Oral Spur

Treat as a cyberspur; use a Special Skill or Quickness for the Melee Combat Test.

Oral Whip

Range equals one meter. Damage is 6M. Use a Special Skill or Quickness for the Ranged Combat Test.

>>>>>(Personally, I'm pleased he ignored the jokes.)<<<<<
—Weasel Boy (03:21:15/12-05-56)

>>>>>(You? I'm impressed.)<<<<<
—Findler-man (12:32:15/12-06-56)

>>>>>(Don't be—he's saving them to use himself.)<<<<<
—Mugger Hugger (21:05:45/12-07-56)

>>>>>(A kiss before dying, perhaps?)<<<<<
—Weasel Boy (21:19:20/12-08-56)

>>>>>(Living up to your name, I see.)<<<<<
—Zoot Suit (02:54:13/12-09-56)

TOOTH COMPARTMENT

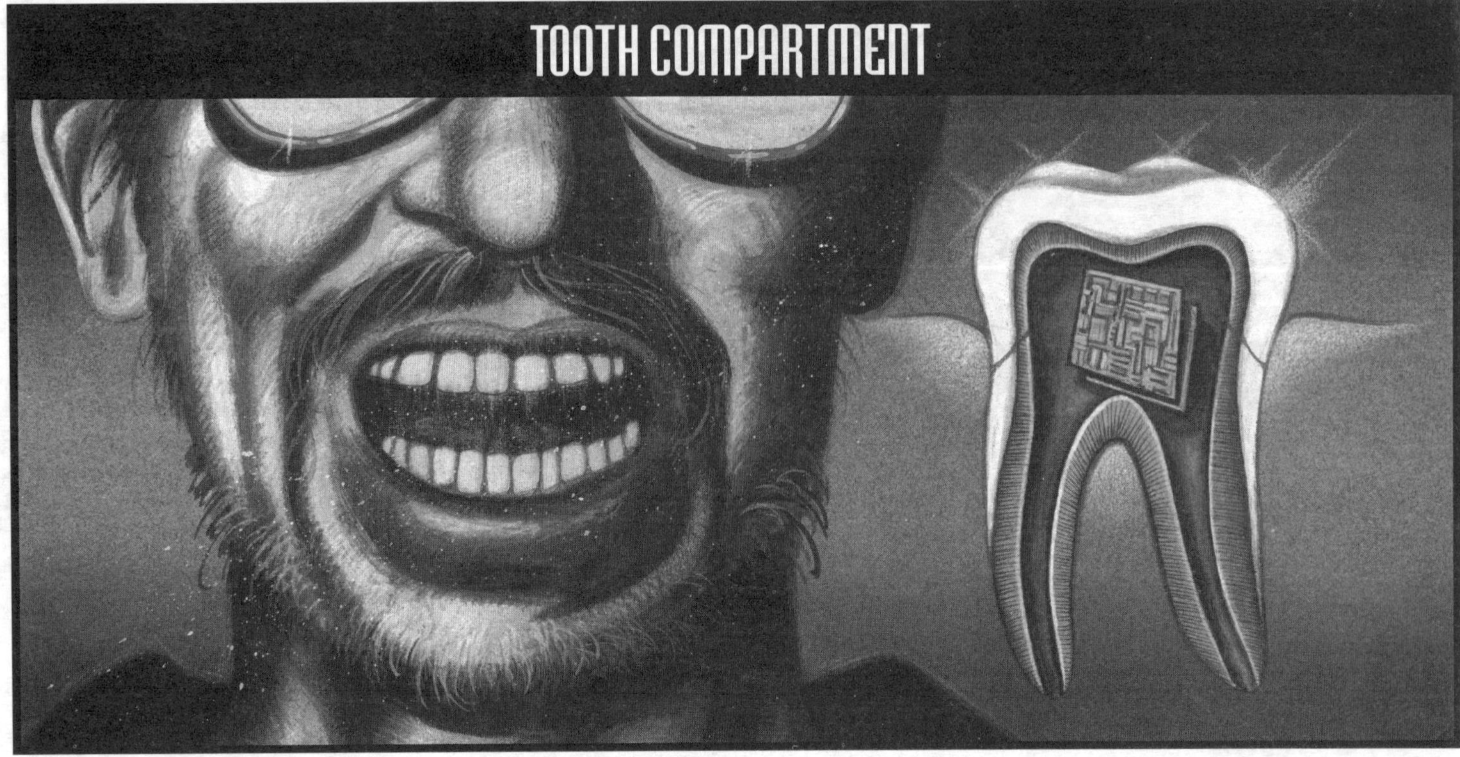

The hollow tooth makes a great place to hide small items or substances. The first model, activated by biting down hard on it, is the one where the spies in all the old movie used to store cyanide. Much better uses in our wonderful century include activating a micro-homing beacon hidden in the tooth, and so on. I know a couple of people with these, and I've never heard of anyone setting one off accidentally.

The second model is for storage only. Microchips are the contraband of choice, though I've heard people use them to smuggle small medical samples and the like. These puppies are in tight so they can't be accidentally knocked out. They can only be removed manually, and that's no easy task. Most compartment teeth are molars or other biggies at the back of the mouth, to keep them out of harm's way.

	Essence Cost	Price	Availability	Street Index
Tooth Compartment				
Breakable	—	700¥	3/48 hrs	1.5
Storage	—	1,500¥	2/48 hrs	1.25

Tooth Compartment

To break the breakable tooth takes a successful Willpower (2) Test if the contents are non-lethal to the user. If the contents are lethal, a Willpower (4) Test is required. Tooth contents take effect immediately. The contents of either type of tooth compartment can be removed or replaced in three minutes.

To remove a storage tooth takes 2 Complex Actions and a successful Quickness (4) Test.

>>>>>(With all those old spy movies to fall back on, you'd think more people would look for fake teeth.)<<<<<
—Findler-man (21:45:10/12-01-56)

>>>>>(Right. The sec-guard at the door of Yamatetsu International's gonna stop people at random and say, "Excuse me, sir. Just let me take a quick look inside your mouth. Won't take a minute!")<<<<<
—Sten (01:42:03/12-02-56)

>>>>>(Nobody watches those old flicks, anyway. Why bother, when you can watch exciting infomercials touting the virtues of the perfect tomato slicer? So much more intellectually enriching!)<<<<<
—Hangfire (23:18:54/12-03-56)

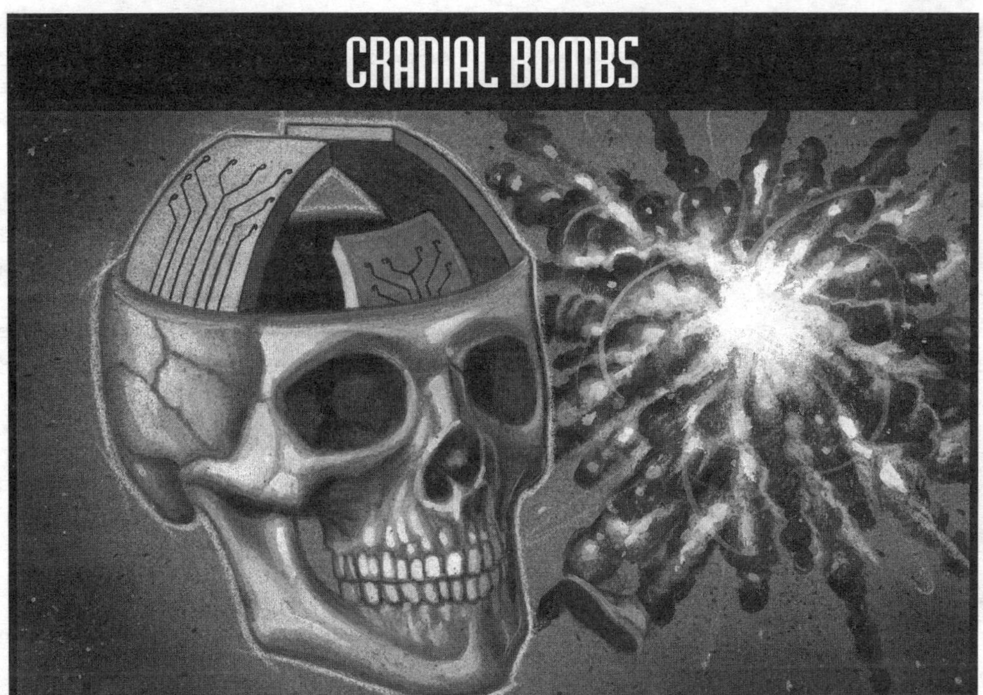

Here's the clean scoop on the ever-popular menace most of us know as the cortex bomb. Lots of people ask me about these nasty things, and I've monitored enough conversation pits in the Matrix to know how little most folks know about them. A cortex bomb is actually just one kind of cranial bomb, placed at the base of or adjacent to the cerebral cortex where its detonation kills the poor slob carrying it. Cranial bombs can also be placed elsewhere for different results (all just fraggin' lovely).

The cranial bomb known on the streets as a kink bomb is a tiny little fragger, and when it goes off you can barely hear it unless it's in your own head. Placed near the cortex, it kills instantly. Placed adjacent to or within headware memory, detonation destroys said cyberbits and usually leaves the poor slob with a king granddaddy of a headache.

A second kind, the microbomb, is just powerful enough to kill the bearer. If you're standing next to him, you'll hear it go off and maybe get hit with some gray matter. The third kind, officially called an area bomb and affectionately known streetside as the cranial nuke, is a piece of high-grade plastic explosive big enough to have a blast radius. This sick puppy kills the bearer and anybody standing too close to him.

Cranial bombs can be remote or time-detonated. I've even heard of c-bombs hooked up to tiny sound-recognition devices. Say the magic word and—BOOM!

	Essence Cost	Price	Availability	Street Index
Cranial Bombs				
Kink Bomb	—	28,000¥	12/14 days	1.5
Microbomb	—	65,500¥	18/48 hrs	1.25
Area Bomb	—	500,000¥	20/14 days	1

Cranial Bombs

If built to do so, all cranial bombs will kill the bearer. At the gamemaster's discretion, kink bombs may have a permanent physiological effect such as blindness, stuttering, and so on. Area bombs can be purchased at Power Levels of 3 through 8 and Damage Levels of M through D. All reduce their blast effects at a rate of –1 per meter. All kill the bearer regardless of blast size.

>>>>>(I was riding the Chicago "L" some years ago—it had just headed underground, I forget where we were—and suddenly BLAM, this guy's head explodes. I was at the far end of the car, but it still knocked me off my feet, smacked the breath out of me, and made my ears ring. Seven people between me and him dampened the blast. Six of them died.

I had an in with Eagle Security at the time. I found out that as far as anyone could tell, his head popped because of a rogue signal in the subway tunnel. Can you imagine?)<<<<<

—Moseby (03:21:45/11-29-56)

>>>>>(Been there, primed that.)<<<<<

—Anderson (03:45:47/12-01-56)

>>>>>(I understand there's a new volatile percussion gel being tested that will pass through most detection equipment. It scans as biomatter on x-rays. Wonderful, neh?)<<<<<

—TylerTerror (02:27:20/12-02-56)

DERMAL PLATING AND SHEATHING

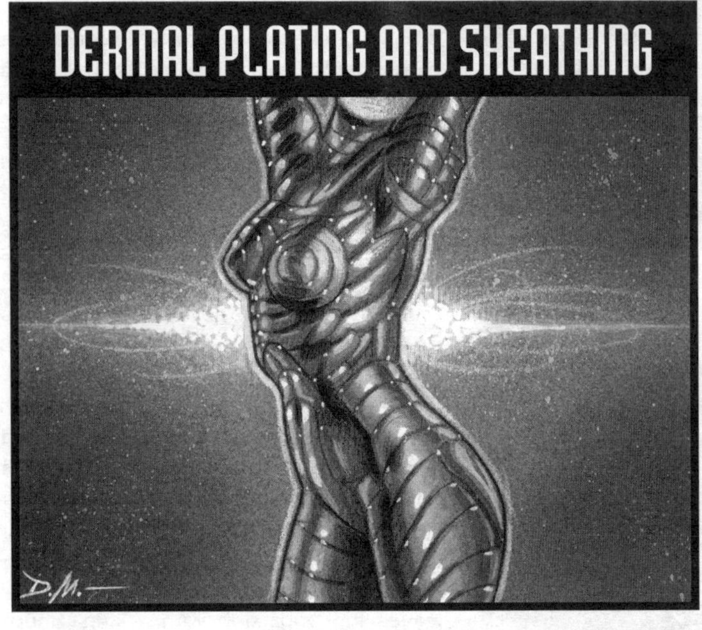

This drek's common on the streets and easier to pick out than you might think. Watch for bunching when the person in question moves. Even the highest-quality, lightest grade sheeting isn't flexible enough to move like skin or muscle. (Orthoskin does, but that's something else again.)

Plenty of people mistakenly think of dermal plating as armor in the same way that an armored jacket is armor. Dermal plating is actually a shock-resistant plastic or semi-metallic fiber weave that distributes some of the energy from impacts—including bullets—over a larger area. Rather than stopping them, it dissipates their kinetic energy as they hit. If you're wearing real armor over your dermals (like any smart sam should), the armor has already slowed the offending object down sufficiently that the plating's small degree of energy dampening actually has an effect.

Users of dermal armor have probably noticed that natural skin doesn't always heal properly where both the skin and the dermal armor have been penetrated. Talk to your street doc about that—he'll know some ways to fix it. One way of dealing with it is to use a new version of dermal plating, known as dermal sheathing, which sidesteps some of the problems. Dermal sheathing combines the latest advances in dermal plating technology with a semi-synthetic skin sheath. The result is smoother and less bulky than standard dermal plating, with greater self-regenerative capability.

Some dermal sheaths use a technology derived from ruthenium polymers, those nifty chem compounds that can change to such a wide array of colors with a small voltaic charge. This sheathing gives you variable coloration within a specified range. To make it sturdy enough to work well as artificial skin, they combined it with something to stiffen it, so it has nowhere near the flexibility of actual ruthenium polymers. The coloration system works for cyberlimbs too, but that version's a little more expensive. Such is the downside of being a chrome god.

	Essence Cost	Price	Availability	Street Index
Dermal Sheath				
Level 1	.7	24,000¥	6/14 days	1.5
Level 2	1.4	60,000¥	6/14 days	1.5
Level 3	2.1	120,000¥	8/14 days	1.5
Coloration Adaptation	—	+50%	+2/+4 days	+.25
Cyber Controller	.1	32,000¥	8/14 days	1.5

Dermal Sheath

The dermal sheath boosts the character's Body Attribute by a number of points equal to the sheath's level plus 1; for example, Level 2 sheathing adds 3 points. It also provides Impact Armor equal to one-half the level, rounded up. Coloration may be purchased as a camouflage pattern (urban, desert, winter, or wilderness), or a solid color (red, green, blue, or black). The coloration intensity can be varied in 10-percent increments using a hand-control or the cyber-controller. Such devices enable the sheath to function as camouflage clothing (see p. 77, **Fields of Fire**).

>>>>>(I saw this drek a few weeks ago, I think, on a hardman in one of the clubs where I slum. He seemed very intent, and being a nosy fragger I kept an eye on him. Never did figure out what he was up to, but I caught sight of him for a moment in good light and noticed an odd sheen to his skin. Almost plastic looking. Dermal sheathing?)<<<<<

—Findler-man (03:44:14/12-02-56)

>>>>>(Maybe. Also could've been artificial skin. It's pretty expensive, but they've been using it for a little while now to treat burn victims who don't have time to wait for vat-grown skin.)<<<<<

—Elias (03:54:46/12-04-56)

>>>>>(Bravo, Elias. Not everything has to do with the biz.)<<<<<

—Findler-man (05:54:37/12-05-56)

FINGERTIP COMPARTMENTS

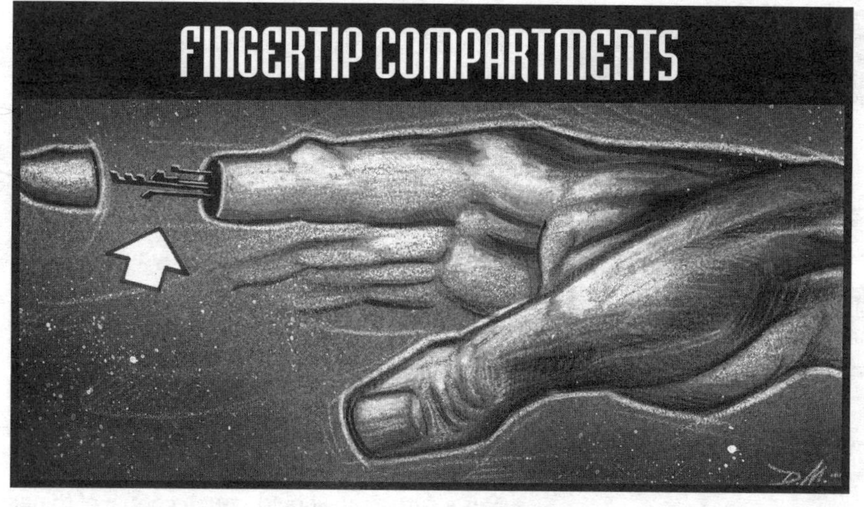

Most people think of fingertip compartments as a place to hide things—especially, god help us, monofilament whips. I won't deny the value of the concealment part. But if you insist on using a monofilament whip, please say to yourself "Hatchetman told me so" when you cut off one of your own limbs—as you eventually will.

A fingertip compartment makes a dandy place for a datajack. For those who want (or need) to keep the presence of their datajack a secret, where better to conceal it? (Don't answer that.) The artificial fingertip plugs nicely into the jack when you don't need to use the ware. Lots of advantages to this one—it's convenient and fast, with no messy wires to string up or trip on. Should an unwanted observer happen to stroll by in mid-operation, it's quicker and less conspicuous to yank your finger out of wherever you've stuck it than to detach and coil a cable.

You can also hide a needle in a fingertip compartment. Built-in drug injectors might be handy in certain sticky situations, neh? You can put pretty much anything you want in that injector, but it can only hold one dose.

Some wizzer fingertip compartments even come with built-in lock picks. Don't think nobody uses lock picks anymore. Even in this age of maglocks and other such devices, simple key-and-tumbler locks are still out there. It can ruin your day to find one, unless you're studly enough to tear it off with your teeth (not likely). The lock pick gizmo is mechanical and comes with a micro-expert system. You pop off the fingertip cover, stick your finger up against the keyhole, and the picks do the rest.

	Essence Cost	Price	Availability	Street Index
Fingertip Datajack		Per standard datajack		
Fingertip ExpertPicks	—	18,000¥	8/2 weeks	3
Fingertip Needle	—	800¥	4/72 hrs	1.5

All of the above require a fingertip compartment; see p. 249, **SRII**.

Fingertip Needle

Holds one dose of any chemical, poison, toxin, or other appropriate compound. To use the needle, a player character must make a successful Unarmed Combat Test. All standard modifiers apply. The needle will not pierce Hardened Armor. Replacing the dose takes two minutes.

Fingertip ExpertPicks

These lock picks have a Skill Rating of 3, and using them is a Complex Action. Most key-and-tumbler locks have a Rating of 2 or 3 depending on their complexity. Resolve attempts to open the lock with an Opposed Test between the lock's rating and that of the ExpertPicks.

>>>>>(I bet there's a bunch of other stuff you can put in a fingertip. Any ideas?)<<<<<

—Mr. Manners (21:12:54/12-01-56)

>>>>>(A gun?)<<<<<

—Mongo (11:08:50/12-02-56)

>>>>>(A single-shot hold-out fingertip pistol, sure. How about a laser link or laser designator? Or a light? Or a taser? Or a camera,or some other kind of media recorder? How about a chemical analyzer, or some sort of toxin sprayer?)<<<<<

—Findler-man (03:12:28/12-05-56)

>>>>>(You think the gun would work?)<<<<<

—Mongo (03:54:24/12-05-56)

CYBERLIMBS

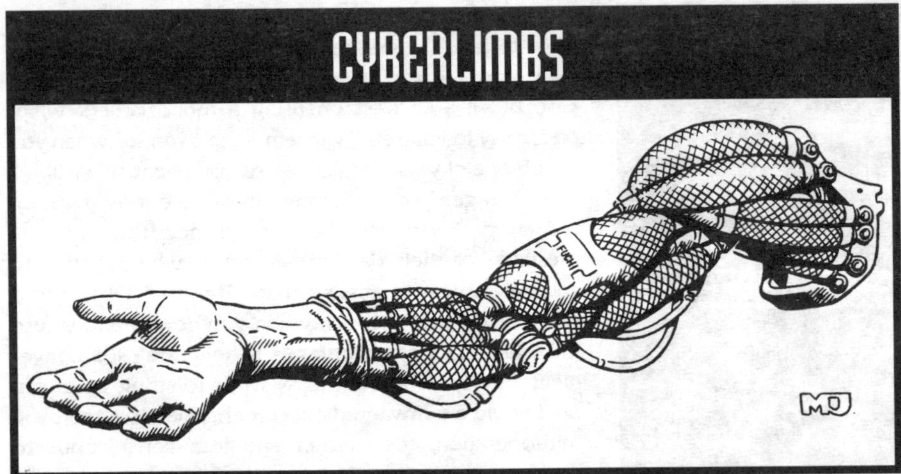

I probably get more questions about cyberlimbs than anything else because there are so many possibilities. I define a cyberlimb as an arm or a leg, or a part of one like a hand, a lower arm, a lower leg, and so on. I'll talk about basic cyberlimbs first, then their possible enhancements. After that, I'll give you chapter and verse about the magnetic cyberlimb system and the cyberarm gyromount (yeah, chumminskis, you read that last one right), a couple of wiz new accessories with which I'm particularly impressed. Next I'll talk weapons, and finally miscellaneous limb accessories. (Once you've read all that, what you don't know about cyberlimbs won't be worth knowing.)

Those of you thinking about getting yourselves a cyberlimb should keep a couple of things in mind. A cyberlimb doesn't work in exactly the same way as a real limb, so it has to be anchored differently. Installing a cyberarm usually involves additional work on the shoulder, while a cyberleg means work on the hip. A partial limb requires a little tinkering with the rest of the arm or leg. Reinforcement is a big part of this work, because cyberlimbs tend to be heavier and stronger than natural limbs. To handle the increased weight and strength, the connecting joints need beefing up.

Also, physical inspections are the tough ones when it comes to keeping your cyberarm a secret. Cyberlimbs look natural to all but the most expert visual inspections, but there's no way to hide that cyberarm or leg from a knowledgeable person who's poking them. Handshakes you can get away with, 'cause lots of people have strong grips. You can also pass through with simple prosthetics most of the time, but the cyberlimbs most shadowfolk like are a little too hard for that.

	Essence Cost	Price	Availability	Street Index
Cyberarm/Leg	1	100,000¥	4/4 days	1
Cyberhand/Foot	.35	45,000¥	3/4 days	1
Cyber Forearm/Lower Leg	.65	70,000¥	4/4 days	1
Semi-natural Covering	—	+10%	Same as limb	1

Cyberlimbs

The presence of a cyberlimb adds to the Power of any unarmed combat attack using that limb. See **General Rules for Cyberlimbs**, p. 49 of **Cyberware Rules**. Also, cyberlimbs reduce Essence loss from some types of cyberware. If the cyberware in question exists entirely in the limb and has minimal neurological connections, the limb offsets Essence loss somewhat.

Semi-natural Covering

This semi-synthetic, natural-looking skin covers the cyberlimb. It adds a +3 modifier to the target number of any visual Perception Tests made to notice the cyberlimb. Note that clothing adds an additional +3 modifier at the gamemaster's discretion, based on how much of the limb is showing.

>>>>>(My left arm is a cyberlimb, and this weird thing happens with it every once in a while. Sometimes I feel like my arm is in a particular position, but when I turn and look it's sitting or hanging completely differently. Freaks me out every time.)<<<<<

—Wanderer (14:28:10/12-04-56)

>>>>>(Phantom limb, that's what they call it. Amputees get it all the time—they can feel the presence of a limb long gone. Some say it's psychological, but I've heard other people say it's your aura remembering the lost limb. I've never heard of anyone getting slotted up because of it, though. It only seems to happen when you're not paying attention to the limb.)<<<<<

—Hangfire (03:21:47/12-05-56)

>>>>>(If this happens with lost limbs, what happens when you get more and more of your body replaced by chrome?)<<<<<

—Weasel Boy (19:57:08/12-06-56)

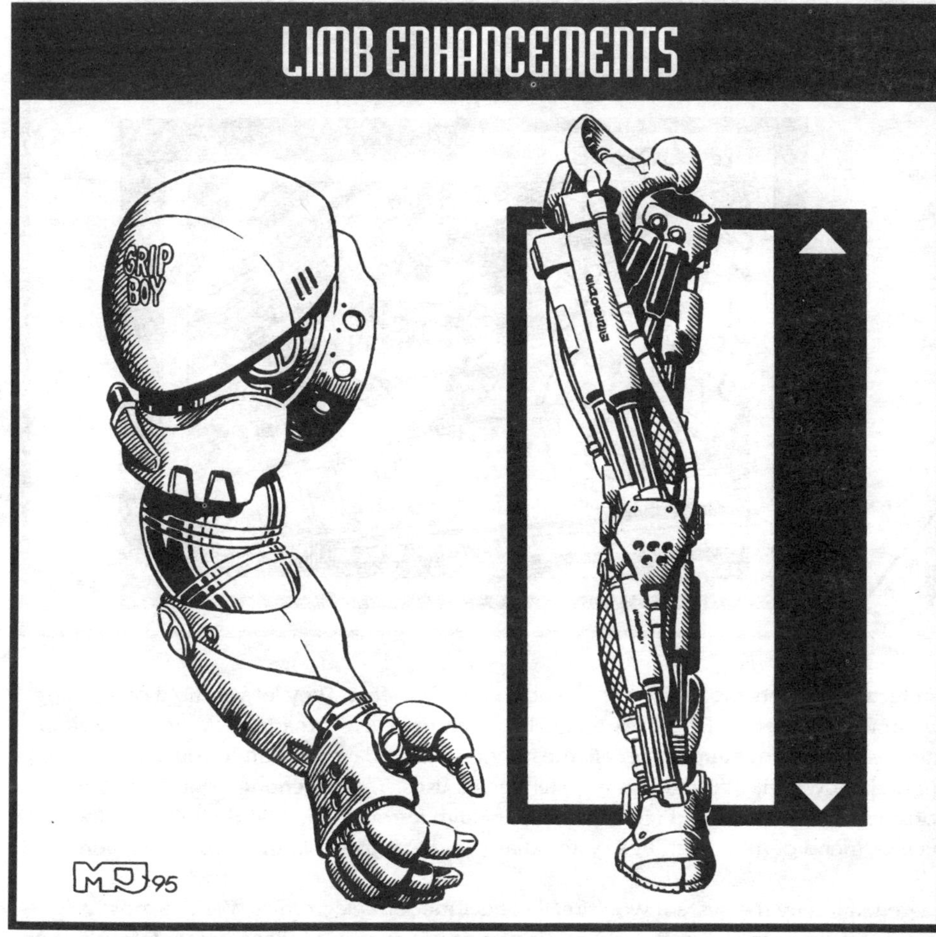

If you're willing to pay, you can get various enhancements for your cyberlimbs to make them stronger, faster and tougher. Enhancements have their limits, however, mostly because of how the various enhancements work together. If you want to make your cyberlimbs stronger, faster *and* tougher all at the same time, you'll end up with one mean piece of chrome for which you'll have paid one nasty hunk of nuyen.

Why the expense? Think about it. I want my limbs stronger, so I pay for heavier lifting servos and more powerful pneumatic and flat-motor systems. That adds weight and bulk. Now that I've got more bulk to move around, making the heavier limb move faster means a major upgrade to the motion servos—which also costs me. To make the limb tougher, I add dermal plating or reinforce it some other way, once again adding weight and bulk and cost, and—you get the idea.

Simple strength, speed, or toughness enhancements are easy enough to handle, up to a point—you pay your nuyen and you take your choice. Once you've beefed up your cyberlimb to the point where its capabilities roughly double the human norm, the cost escalates, especially if you want anything that looks even remotely human. If you can live with decidedly cyber-looking cyberlimbs, however, you have no problem.

	Essence Cost	Price	Availability	Street Index
Strength Enhancement				
1–3 points (per limb)	—	150,000¥/point	6/4 days	1.5
4+ points (per limb)	.4/point	175,000¥/point	6/4 days	1.5
Quickness Enhancement				
1–3 points (per limb)	—	90,000¥/point	8/4 days	1.5
4+ points (per limb)	.3/point	110,000¥/point	8/4 days	1.5
Body Enhancement	—	75,000¥/point	6/4 days	1.5

>>>>>(I don't know how many cyberlimbs old Hatchetboy has, but I've got four plus some torso mods, and keeping it all balanced is a pain in the ass! Everything is naturally balanced on the human body, but us cybered folk can get speed enhancements or some such to just one limb. Sound wiz, you think? Try again. It doesn't work too well for things like coordination and balance. I don't want to think about the number of hours I've spent hooked up to diagnostic gear getting the settings tweaked.)<<<<<

—Street Knight (21:18:32/11-29-56)

>>>>>(Is it worth it?)<<<<<

—Weasel Boy (03:54:19/12-05-56)

>>>>>(If you ever end up on the wrong side of me, you'll find out.)<<<<<

—Street Knight (18:25:46/12-06-56)

MAGNETIC CYBERLIMB SYSTEM

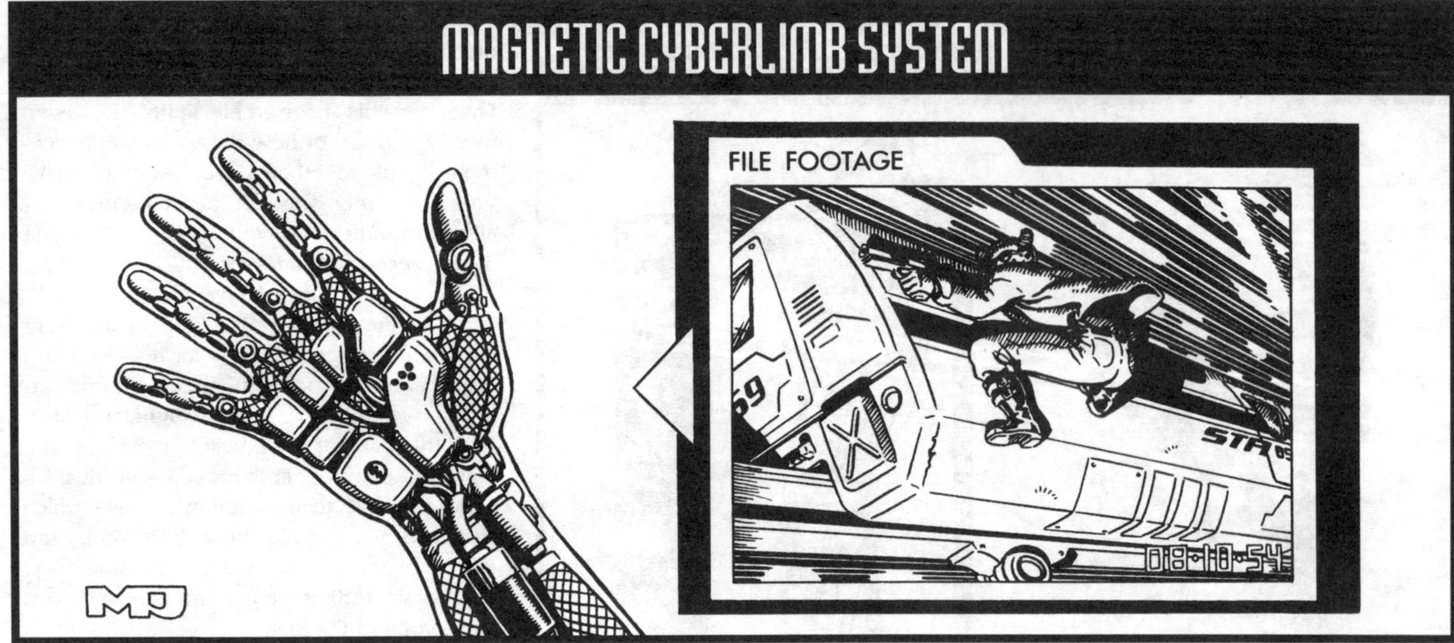

This system for cyberarms and legs is a series of electro-magnets mounted in the hands, knees and feet. They let you hold on to things better—metal things, that is, specifically things made of ferrous metals. (The drek that cyberware and such is made of is right out, chummeroo. Sorry.) With that limitation, some people might pass this gadget up—after all, most metals these days are non-ferrous. In fact, most "metals" are actually a semi-metallic polymer compound. However, the mag system still has its uses. There's enough out there that you can grab onto to make it worth having. Lots of vehicles, especially trucks and big cars, have enough ferrous metal. So do buildings (beams, supports and so on), railings, support cables, and such. A friend of mine with this system has put metal plates in the grips of his guns and other weapons. He doesn't drop them anymore.

Sorry to tell you, though, that the magnetic field generated by the system won't really affect modern electronics. We use mostly light-optics these days—you might be able to mess with the power supply, but the effect won't amount to much. These magnets can't even erase optical chips.

	Essence Cost	Price	Availability	Street Index
Magnetic Cyberlimb System (per cyberlimb)	—	2,800¥	6/7 days	2

Magnetic Cyberlimb System

Each limb system can only hold about 25 kilograms. Multiple systems are cumulative. The weight the magnets can hold is subtracted from the weight of anything being held (see **Dangling and Holding**, p. 51 of **Cyberware Rules**).

>>>>>(I'm the friend Hatchetman's talking about who's got the magnetic system (at least, I think I am), and it's saved my metal hide more than once. In one case—and please don't ask me to go into specifics—I hung onto the bottom of a Banshee t-bird as it hard-balled across the desert. Not fun, but I'm alive.)<<<<<
—Steel Lynx (22:15:20/12-01-56)

>>>>>(Wait a minute, a Banshee's armor is a ceramic compound! That's not ferrous by a long shot. I smell bulldrek here.)<<<<<
—Weasel Boy (03:41:17/12-02-56)

>>>>>(The only drek you smell is your brain, Weasel-dude. There's enough metal under there if you know where to stick your hand, or if the vehicle in question was kind enough to take an AVM in the gut before you latched on to it.)<<<<<
—Steel Lynx (14:08:58/12-04-56)

CYBERARM GYROMOUNT

Here's the one the sammie boys are twitchin' in the street for—a gyromount IN YOUR ARM. Pretty wiz, neh? Some bunch of bright techboys brought this puppy to market about six weeks ago, so we are talking white-drek-hot. Talk about improving your firing capability—better balance, nowhere near as much recoil from big nasty guns—a fraggin' beautiful piece of 'ware. Want to know the best part? It works just like a regular cyberarm! You can enhance it and play with it and do pretty much whatever you like to it. Okay, now for the drawbacks. First, don't even think about hiding the fact that this is a cyberarm. The pair of counterweights that come out near the wrist when you start to rock-and-roll are a dead giveaway, believe me. Also, it costs *a lot* of nuyen. This thing costs BIG 'cause it's new and you all want it. You REALLY want it, you've got to pay for it. Go find a gold mine, folks.

Here's one more thing you'll find useful with a cyberarm gyromount, or any other wiz piece of hardware you choose to stick in your limbs—the direct neural interface. This ever-so-handy device passes data directly from a piece of gear in a cyberarm to your brain, giving you cybernetic control of your gyromount/gun/whatever.

	Essence Cost	Price	Availability	Street Index
Cyberarm Gyromount	1.5	260,000¥	10/21 days	2
Direct Neural Interface	.1	4,500¥	4/6 days	1

Gyromount Cyberarm

This piece of cyberware works like a standard gyromount and provides 3 points of recoil reduction. It can be used with any weapon up to and including a light machine gun.

Direct Neural Interface

Allows cybernetic control of any device not originally designed to be cybernetically controlled that is placed in a cyberlimb, at a 50 percent increase in the device's cost.

>>>>>(Yup yup, gyromount arms. Been waiting for this baby. Time to get the old arms hacked off. Yup. Yup.)<<<<<
—Weasel Boy (21:18:54/12-01-56)

>>>>>(Is he serious?)<<<<<
—Tyger (03:22:54/12-02-56)

>>>>>(Who knows?)<<<<<
—WHOEVER (05:33:52/12-01-56)

OTHER CYBERLIMB ACCESSORIES

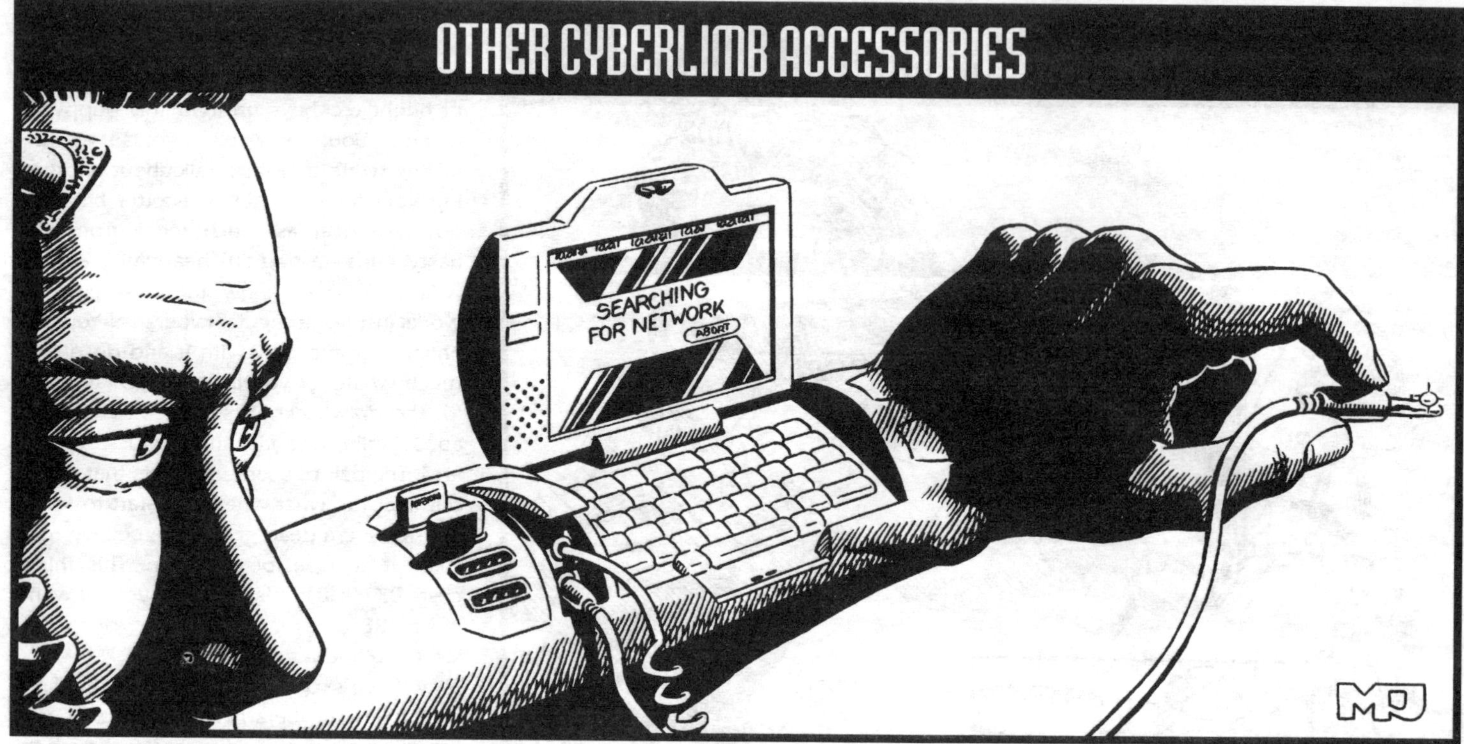

You have the foot spur, replacement hand, and cyberarm cyberdeck to consider. The foot spur shoots down through the heel of the cyberfoot. You can stab somebody with it or anchor yourself to the ground. How well it works depends on what kind of ground you're shooting it into. You can get a foot spur for your regular foot, but lots of work has to be done to your ankles and shins so your bones don't just snap off near the blade when pressure is applied.

You see replacement hands in all the stupid trid shows, and I think they belong there. Still, some people must think it's wiz to have a hand with a Walther PPK already in it. Me, I'd rather take the half-second to pick up whatever I need.

The cyberarm cyberdeck is a deck you can install in your cyberarm. Deckers probably love this one. I'm not a decker, so I don't care about it. You can also get tactical computers and orientation systems installed in a cyberarm; both are incredibly useful.

	Essence Cost	Price	Availability	Street Index
Foot Anchor	.4	14,000¥	6/7 days	2
Replacement Hand	—	28,000¥	12/14 days	2
Cyberarm Cyberdeck	—	Varies*	Varies*	NA
Tactical Computer				
Level 1	3.5	350,000¥	12/60 days	4
Level 2	4.0	900,000¥	12/60 days	4
Level 3	4.5 (Estimated)	CLASSIFIED	CLASSIFIED	CLASSIFIED
Level 4	5 (Estimated)	CLASSIFIED	CLASSIFIED	CLASSIFIED
Orientation System	.5	15,000¥	5/6 days	1.5

*See **Cyberarm Cyberdeck**, p. 36.

Foot Anchor

As a weapon, the foot spur does (STR–1)M Damage. As an anchor, it cannot penetrate materials with a Barrier Rating higher than 8, the Barrier Rating of most pavement. Each foot anchored increases the amount of weight a character can hold up or hang on to by a maximum of 50 kilograms. If the foot anchor is set into a material with a Barrier Rating of less than 8, each Barrier Rating point below 8 reduces the amount of weight by 5 kilograms. See **Dangling and Holding**, p. 51 of **Cyberware Rules**.

Replacement Hand

Attaching/removing a replacement hand requires a free hand and a Complex Action. A variety of tool and gear/weapon hands are available, at a 30-percent increase of the cost of the item itself. Weapons built into a replacement hand receive a +1 modifier to the target number for purposes of Combat Tests.

OTHER CYBERLIMB ACCESSORIES

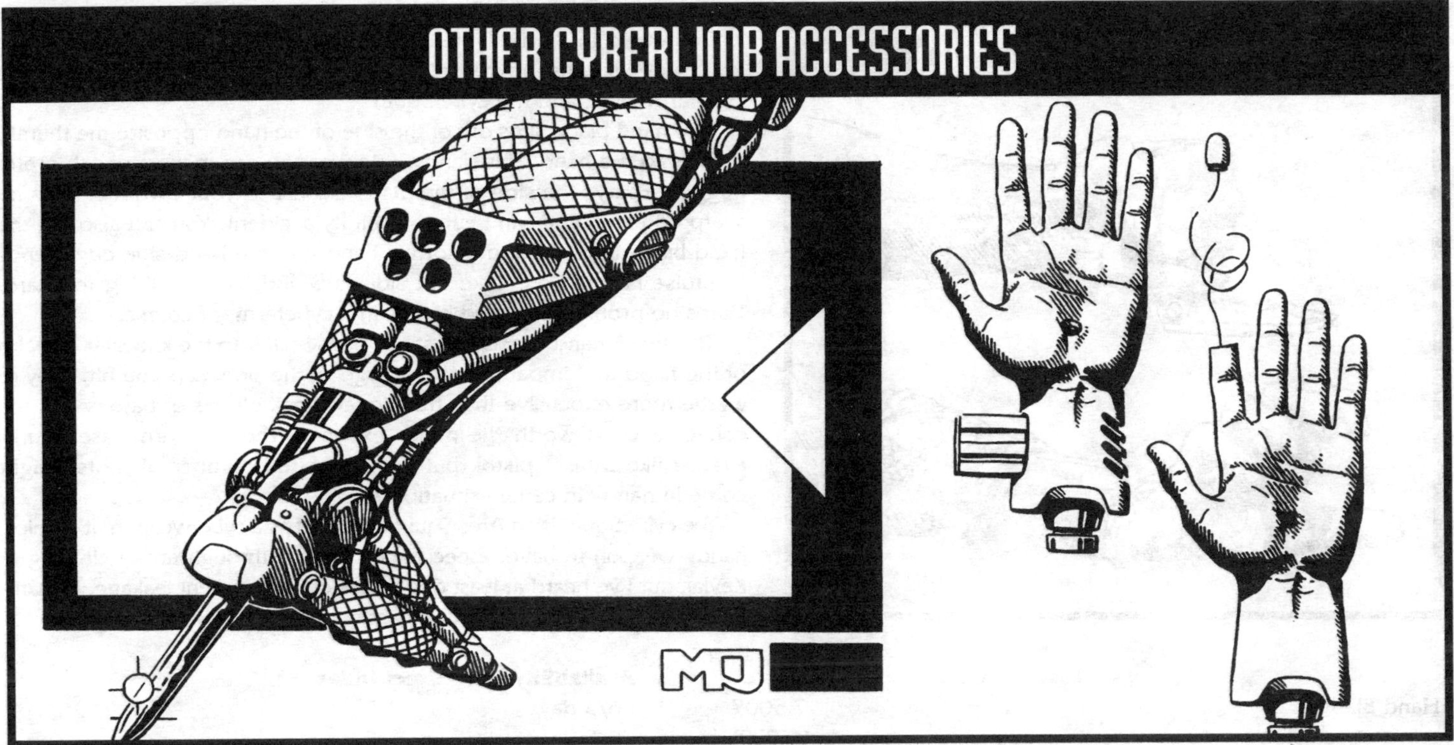

Cyberarm Cyberdeck

Players may install standard or cranial cyberdecks in cyberarms. For standard decks, multiply the price of the selected deck by 4, increase the Availability target number by 25 percent (round up), and double the Base Time for acquiring it. See p. 38, **Shadowtech**, for rules on installing a cranial cyberdeck in the arm. Increase the standard target number for building each component by +2, and increase costs and Base Times per component by 20 percent .

Tactical Computer/Orientation System

Cyberarm versions of these pieces of equipment work in the same way as cranial versions (pp. 53 and 63 of **Shadowtech**, respectively).

>>>>>(The only thing I've ever seen a replaceable cyberhand used for is—never mind.)<<<<<
—Friggy (21:18:40/11-29-56)

>>>>>(Hey, joker, wanna meet me and my Predator II hand for a little quickdraw? Bet I win.)<<<<<
—Tuff (18:35:24/11-30-56)

>>>>>(A word of advice to anyono who gets the foot anchor— DON'T TRY HOLDING BACK A CAR! Trust me, the result is VERY painful.)<<<<<
—Corpus Delicious (21:55:09/12-01-56)

>>>>>(I know a bunch of deckers who've gone for the cyberdeck in the cyberarm. Personally, I think it's a little risky, but it's not my couple-hundred-thousand-nuyen piece of hardware.)<<<<<
—Findler-man (03:44:10/12-03-56)

>>>>>(The cyberarm deck is a step up from hauling a regular deck around, but I'm not sure it's any better than the cranial cyberdeck.)<<<<<
—White Tiger (23:28:46/12-06-56)

CYBERLIMB WEAPONS

Most of you folks reading this already know about the weapons usually mounted in a cyberlimb: spurs, razors, and cyberguns. I know of a few more (surprise, surprise!): the hand blade, the shock hand, the cyberarm taser, and the cyberSquirt.

The hand blade slips out of the side of the hand opposite the thumb, parallel to the hand. This dandy little weapon can make a punch pretty fragging nasty. The side of the blade closest to your own hand has no sharp edge, so you can't cut yourself by accident. You can also get the hand blade implanted in a normal hand, but the hand-side edge tends to bruise flesh if you strike out sideways and hit something too hard. That's no problem for hand blades in a cyberarm, of course.

The shock hand consists of shock pads built into the knuckles or palm of the hand that impart a nasty charge to the poor sap you hit. They're a little more expensive than traditional shock gloves or batons, but the convenience is worth the minor expense. The cyberarm taser works exactly like a taser pistol, but with a limited number of shots. Might come in handy in certain situations.

The cyberSquirt is an Ares Squirt mounted as a cyberweapon. It's a nice, handy weapon to have, especially for getting through armor clothing or Kevlar, but I've heard at least one report of containment leakage. Be careful with this one—dosing yourself accidentally can really ruin your day.

	Essence Cost	Price	Availability	Street Index
Hand Blade	.1	7,500¥	6/5 days	1.5
Retractable	.25	10,000¥	6/5 days	1.5
Shock Hand	—	1,300¥	6/4 days	2
Cyberarm Taser	—	2,000¥	6/4 days	1.5
CyberSquirt	—	1,400¥	8/6 days	2

Hand Blades

Hand blades do (STR + 3)L Damage. Essence Cost only applies if the blade is mounted in a normal hand.

Shock Hand and Cyberarm Taser

The shock hand does 8S Damage and holds 12 charges. It must be recharged after 12 uses The cyberarm taser does 10S Damage, but can fire only two shots before recharging. It has the same ranges as the standard taser (p. 103, **SRII**).

CyberSquirt

The cyberSquirt fires up to 10 shots at a time of chemical/biological agents in a special gelling agent. Like the non-cybered Ares Squirt, the cyberSquirt holds 10 chemical rounds and the gel reservoir holds enough gel for up to 20 shots. The reservoir must be reloaded once for every 2 cartridge reloads. The gel is made of DMSO (dimethyl sulfoxide), a utility chemical that forces the skin to absorb delivered chemical/biological agents. Porous armor, such as armor clothing and Kevlar weaves, offers no protection against DMSO. Rigid armor (higher than 5, or plated) applies half its normal Defensive Rating (rounded up) against DMSO attacks. (See p. 92, **Shadowtech**, for effects of DMSO.)

>>>>>(Flexibility is the key, people. The more options you have at any one time, the better off you are. Limited choices mean limited opportunities.)<<<<<
—Findler-man (03:14:47/12-02-56)

>>>>>(Geez, usually you gotta pay loads for that kind of advice.)<<<<<
—Measle (10:54:48/12-03-56)

>>>>>(By the way, gents, an insulated cyberhand will protect you from the zap of an electric fence.)<<<<<
—Sten (21:18:59/12-05-56)

CYBERTORSOS AND SKULLS

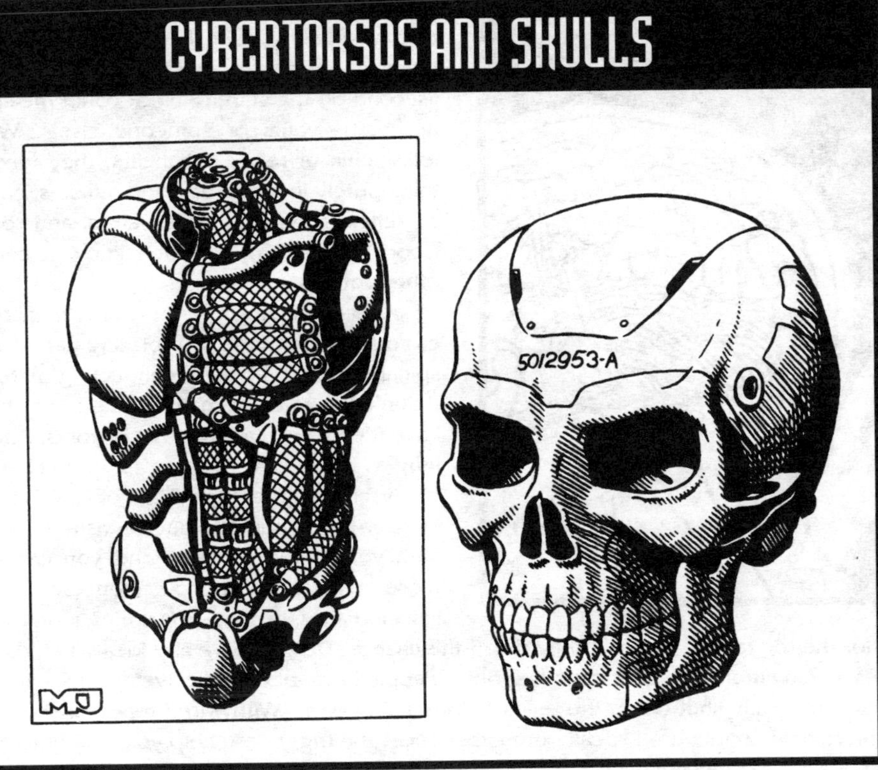

Here's a scary thought—a cyber-body and a cyber-head to go with your cyberarms and legs. Hardly enough warm human flesh left to bother with, is there? The perfect mechanism, driven by a human brain and soul. Better than God made, 'cause we can fix the Cyber Man a lot easier.

The doctors and scientists here talk about this a lot. They think I'm not listening, that the music coming over my headset drowns out their words. But I can hear them. It scares me. But listening to the nurses scares me even more. The doctors are clinical, scientific. The nurses call it like they see it. You know what they call Cyber Man? A zombie.

You don't need to know about that. You need to know about the cybertorso and the cyberskull. They act as framework and protection for various other cybersystems, kind of like how our real torsos and skulls protect our vulnerable insides.

Body plating can give you more protection if you want it. Ceramic and hybrid-polymer plating replaces the outer casing of your various cyber body parts, as soft armor or hardened armor depending on how much you've got to spend.

	Essence Cost	Price	Availability	Street Index
Cybertorso	1.5	120,000¥	6/4 days	1
Cyberskull	.75	75,000¥	6/4 days	1
Body Plating				
Soft Armor	—	10,000¥/level	12/2 weeks	2
Hard Armor	—	25,000¥/level	14/3 weeks	2

Cybertorso and Cyberskull

The cybertorso and cyberskull each add +1 to the character's Body Attribute. The cybertorso also reduces by half (round up) the additional Essence cost of Strength or Quickness enhancements beyond 3 points (see **Limb Enhancements**, p. 31, and **Cyberware Rules**, p. 49).

Body Plating

Soft armor adds 1 point of Ballistic and Impact armor per level, cumulative with any armor worn. Hard armor also adds 1 point of Ballistic and Impact armor per level, but functions as hardened armor per the critter power Hardened Armor (p. 218, **SRII**.) Body plating can also be applied to cyberlimbs. See also **Armor,** p. 49 of **Cyberware Rules**.

>>>>>(Oh man, I think I'm starting to figure out what's happening to Hatchetman!)<<<<<
—Weasel Boy (22:09:53/12-02-56)

>>>>>(They can't be serious! Replace his whole body?! Spirits above—that's insane! Isn't' it?)<<<<<
—Findler-man (03:54:19/12-03-56)

>>>>>(I thought so when I got this drek, but now I'm not so sure. I did some research and pulled in some favors, and it seems they are replacing Hatchetman's body. We all thought that was impossible—seems we were wrong.)<<<<<
—Captain Chaos (10:57:36/12-06-56)

WIRED REFLEX SYSTEMS

Some people say—and I'm one of them—that a street samurai lives and dies by his reflexes. Edge is everything. That extra millisecond off the starting block could mean life or death—yours or someone else's. When folks think of reflex enhancers, they tend to think purely in terms of wired reflexes, boosted reflexes, synaptic accelerators, and so on. Good ware, all of it—but I know a couple other options.

A reaction enhancer, for example, increases your reaction time by replacing part of your spinal column with superconducting material. I don't know what material they use, but I have friends who tell me that it works. And as long as it works, who cares about much else?

A reflex trigger is a variant of wired reflexes. Get this cybernetic device installed along with your wired reflexes, and you can turn those reflexes on and off. (You can't get it installed after the fact—the wiring won't work right.) I know a bunch of people who'd have gone for the trigger like a shot if they'd had the chance. Do you have any idea what it's like to go through normal life wired to the max? Reflexes are an automatic, instinctive response. People have lots of reflexive actions—fight or flight, for example—but if they have to, the unwired can usually shut down the reflex before acting on it. With wired reflexes, you can't always manage that. Sometimes that can result in unfortunate accidents—I speak from experience. The trigger can help you avoid that kind of thing. If you're contemplating wires, get a trigger. It's a good investment.

	Essence Cost	Price	Availability	Street Index
Reaction Enhancer	.3/point	60,000¥	6/7 days	2
Reflex Trigger	+.2	+13,000¥	As wired reflexes	

Reaction Enhancers

Player characters may increase Reaction up to a maximum of +6 in this manner. The reaction enhancer is completely compatible with all other reaction/Initiative boosters except the move-by-wire system (see p. 39) and the adrenal pump (p. 19, **Shadowtech**).

Reflex Trigger

Activating or deactivating wired reflexes with a reflex trigger requires a Simple Action. For additional information, see **Effects of Wired Reflexes**, p. 53 of **Cyberware Rules**.

>>>>>(I've seen some unfortunate things happen with wired reflexes, especially around street punks who've just gotten the wire and aren't used to it. One false move, one loud noise, and BANG!)<<<<<
—Hangfire (03:45:18/12-02-56)

>>>>>(I had to work with a joker like that for a while. I kept threatening to dose him with MAO if he didn't relax. I finally had to, the bastard.)<<<<<
—Findler-man (23:18:59/12-04-56)

>>>>>(I actually had my wire taken out and put back in with a reflex trigger. Couldn't stand being on the edge all the time. It was literally making me crazy.)<<<<<
—Steel Lynx (00:21:47/12-06-56)

>>>>>(What is this, a therapy circle?)<<<<<
—Wacko Deluxe (21:21:49/12-07-56)

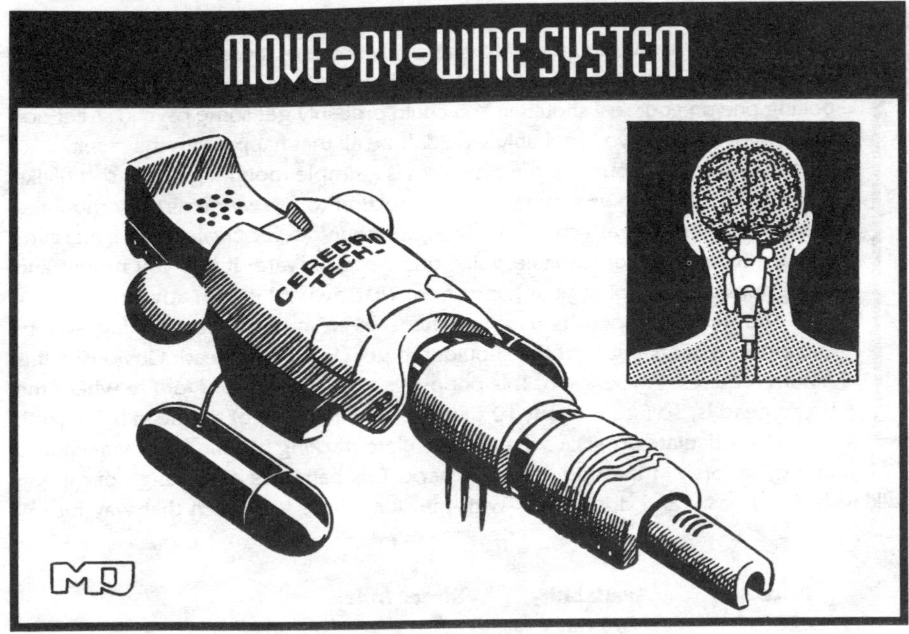

This wiz piece of wire needs a little background explanation. Modern aircraft and some other kinds of vehicles (t-birds mostly) use what's known as a fly-by-wire system. As I've heard it explained, the design of the aircraft is inherently unstable. It literally wants to fly in all directions at once. The fly-by-wire system keeps it under control by using a series of redundant computers that continually counteract the chaotic motion of the craft. This also means that when the craft is told to move in a specific direction, it already wants to do that, and so is much more responsive and maneuverable. Imagine applying this to a person, and you've got the move-by-wire system.

As I understand it, this system puts your body in a constant state of seizure. A computer in your brain monitors the state of the seizure and counteracts its effects until you tell it that you want to move. At that point it channels the effects of the seizure along the motion path desired.

This system lets you move with unnatural smoothness. Move-by-wire makes someone with mere balance augmentation look spastic. You can spot the joker with move-by-wire a mile off. There's another giveaway too, which I suspect will disappear once they perfect the technology. Every once in a while the person with a move-by-wire system develops a slight tremor in one muscle group. It's not as obvious as a twitch or spasm, but you can see it if you're looking for it or at it. As far as I know, the tremor only hits when the muscle group is at rest. If it's in motion, everything's fine. I figure it has something to do with built-in errors when the system's compensating for the seizure, but don't quote me on that.

	Essence Cost	Price	Availability	Street Index
Move-by-Wire System				
Level 1	2.5	250,000¥	8/10 days	2.5
Level 2	3.85	500,000¥	12/20 days	3
Level 3	5.2	1,250,000¥	18/30 days	3
Level 4	6.45	3,000,000¥	20/45 days	3.5

Move-by-Wire System

The move-by-wire system provides the following benefits at each level. This system is not compatible with any other Reaction/Initiative enhancing cyber- or bioware.

Level 1: +1 Quickness, +2 Reaction, +1D6 Initiative, +1 die for Athletics and Stealth tests
Level 2: +2 Quickness, +4 Reaction, +2D6 Initiative, +2 dice for Athletics and Stealth tests
Level 3: +3 Quickness, +6 Reaction, +3D6 Initiative, +3 dice for Athletics and Stealth tests
Level 4: +4 Quickness, +8 Reaction, +4D6 Initiative, +4 dice for Athletics and Stealth tests

>>>>>(Oh man oh man oh man!)<<<<<
—Droog Hopeful (23:19:20/12-02-56)

>>>>>(This thing puts you in a continuous seizure??! A seizure is a sign of severe neurological dysfunction! That's insane! What are the long-term effects? Does anyone have any idea??)<<<<<
—Findler-man (21:29:33/12-03-56)

>>>>>(I'm with you, Findler, but I can see where some people might want it. The end result is pretty impressive. As for long-term effects, does anyone really know what any of this cyberdrek will do to you after a couple years?)<<<<<
—Hangfire (03:54:48/12-04-56)

WEAPON MOUNTS

Here's some red meat for the round-the-bend hard boys out there: external mounts, tracking mounts, and articulate arms. Some of these mounts can only go on a cyberlimb or cybertorso, thank fraggin' whoever, so don't even think about bolting one on your real shoulder. You could probably get some psycho street doc to do it for you, but you probably wouldn't be all that happy with the result.

The external mount for the cyberarm is a simple mounting point, sort of like a hardpoint, that allows a cybernetic connection to a weapon already mounted there. The guns that attach to the external mount are equivalents of cyberguns and are fully smartgun-capable. I like this piece of ware; it lets you mount and use a gun while keeping your hands free. *That's* what I call an advantage.

The tracking mount is usually connected to an eye laser tracking system and extends at an angle off the shoulder to get clear of the head. Obviously, this mount requires a cybertorso. This puppy also has a dead spot for fire where the user's head is, so figure about 10 degrees to either side of the head is blocked.

The articulate arm is a separate articulate tracking mount, usually anchored to a cybertorso in the middle of the back. This baby has a full range of motion and can cover fragging near any firing angle. We're talking big and nasty and don't-mess-with-me. It's a little too much that way for my taste, but the hard-edged razorboys ought to lap it up.

	Essence Cost	Price	Availability	Street Index
External Mount	—	3,200¥	6/4 days	2
Tracking Mount	—	24,000¥	8/7 days	2
Articulate Arm	.25	110,000¥	12/24 days	2

External Mount

Attaching or detaching a weapon from this mount requires a Complex Action. The mount takes light, heavy, or machine pistols and submachine guns; double the cost of the weapon. Player characters can buy external ammo pods that hold 50 rounds, but only one pod can be mounted at any given time. For quadruple the listed price, the mount can be made to retract into a cyberarm that has had a Body enhancement of at least +1.

Tracking Mount

This mount is a motorized, pivoting tracking system that ties into an eye laser designator. It can take light, heavy, or machine pistols, submachine guns, and assault rifles; triple the cost of the weapon. Player characters can buy external ammo pods that hold 50 rounds, but only one pod can be mounted at any given time. The system gives users 3 points of Recoil Reduction, plus the same modifiers as a laser sight.

Articulate Arm

This mount works like a tracking mount, but has a full range of motion and covers a 360-degree firing area. The articulate arm can take all light weapons up to a light machine gun. The system gives users 3 points of Recoil Reduction, plus the same modifiers as a laser sight.

>>>>>(This articulate thingamawhosis is an arm?)<<<<<
—Happy Go Lately (21:45:20/12-02-56)

>>>>>(No, not really. It looks a lot like the arm on a gyromount, except it attaches to your back and extends high enough to reach over your head. It can pan over 360 degrees and has 120 degrees of motion at the mounting point and the primary joint. Impressive coverage.)<<<<<
—Hangfire (03:54:02/12-05-56)

>>>>>(So anybody with all of this stuff is pretty much a walking tank.)<<<<<
—Colonel Cobra (05:55:48/12-05-56)

>>>>>(Yup. And I think Hatchetman will be—or is, by now—the first.)<<<<<
—Findler-man (03:54:48/12-06-56)

>>>>>(No, not the first.)<<<<<
—Nightfire (05:22:46/12-06-56)

MISCELLANEOUS CYBERWARE

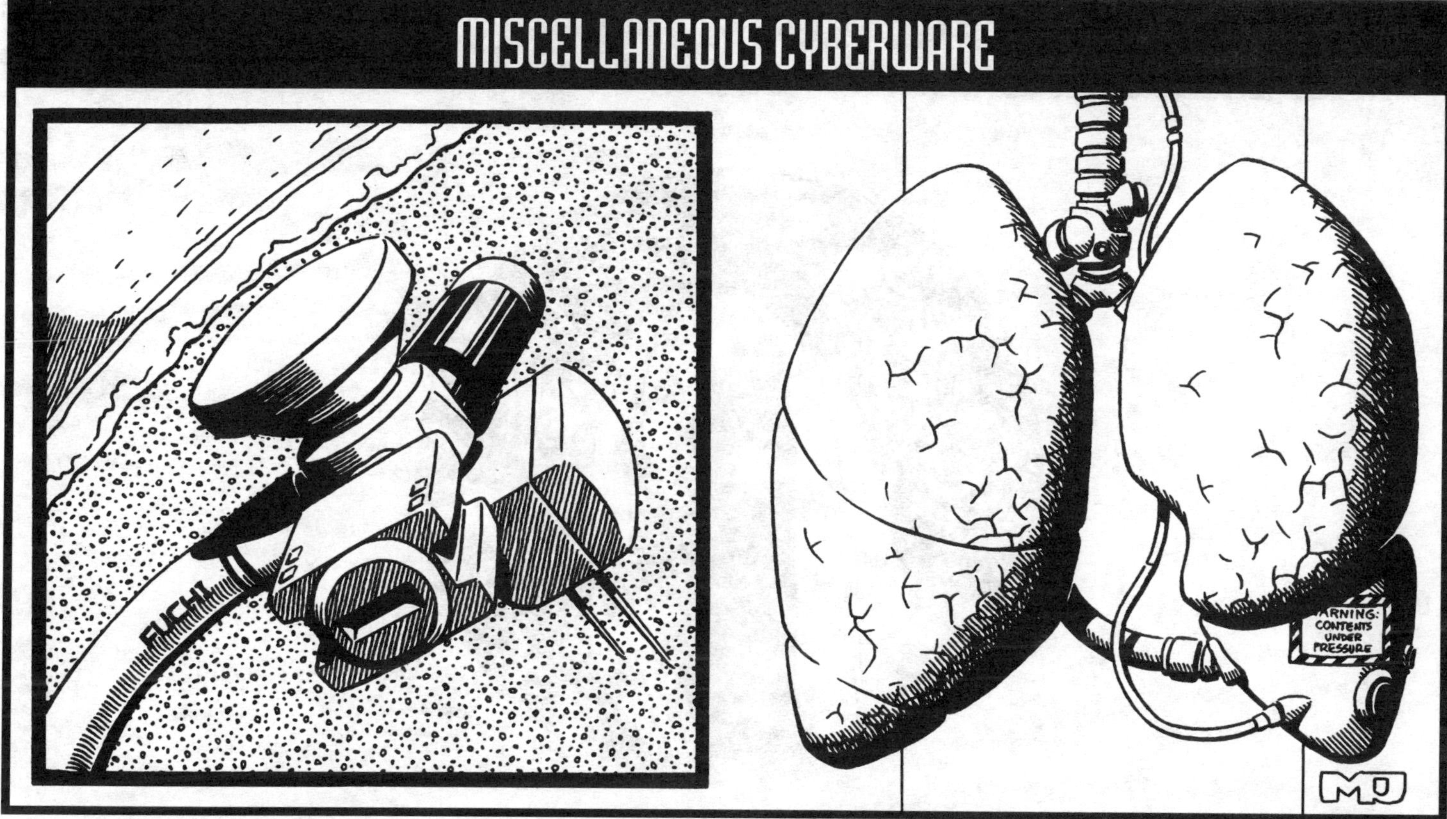

Here's a couple of odd pieces: the induction datajack and the internal air tank. Anybody jumping around and getting all loopy over the induction datajack, calm down. It's a wizzer little toy, but it does *not* allow you to grab a wire or put your hand on a computer and suck up data from it. This jack is a subdermal induction pad. You can attach a cable and a special induction connector between it and the standard data-out port on a cyberdeck or computer and then use it just like a standard datajack. Because it's under the skin, it can't be seen, so you can jander into places that might be harder to crack if the security guard saw a bright silver datajack at your temple.

The internal air tank is exactly what it sounds like—an independent air source. While breathing from it, you are immune to any inhalable toxin or sleepy gas or other compound. The tank only holds about twenty minutes' worth of air, so don't stay anywhere dangerous for too long. Refilling it takes five minutes.

	Essence Cost	Price	Availability	Street Index
Induction Datajack	.3	3,000¥	5/4 days	2
Internal Air Tank	.25	1,200¥	4/5 days	1.5

Induction Datajack

Performs identically to standard and improved datajacks (p. 246 of **SRII** and p. 45 of **Shadowtech**, respectively). For the induction equivalent to the datajacks listed in **Shadowtech**, add .1 to the Essence, multiply the Price by 3, and use the Availability/Street Index listed above.

Air Tank

The internal air tank can be vented if necessary.

>>>>>(I got an air tank, but I fill it with propane and I carry a lighter.)<<<<<
—Worm (23:09:58/12-04-56)

>>>>>(Shut up, Worm.)<<<<<
—Findler-man (23:17:10/12-05-56)

CYBERWARE RULES

Cyberware Rules provides revised and expanded rules for various pieces of cybertechnology in the **Shadowrun** game. Some of these have been described in previous sourcebooks—others are new. The rules in this section deal with some of the pros and cons of cyberware in greater detail than in previously published sourcebooks, so that gamemasters can enrich their gaming sessions by bringing additional elements into play. This section does not attempt to give detailed rules for every possible situation in which cyberware may be used, but rather offers broad guidelines.

In all instances where material in this section contradicts previously published material, the newer material should take precedence, but the gamemaster ultimately decides which version to use. As always, the name of the game is fun and the gamemaster is the final arbiter. Gamemasters should keep in mind, however, that an over-chromed campaign can become unbalanced and dull very quickly. If the gamemaster wants to limit his players' ability to obtain or use certain pieces of cybertech, he can make those items unavailable, horrendously expensive, or otherwise undesirable. For example, the clinic that outfits the runners with the forbidden ware may sell them inferior gear and then go out of business. Alternatively, he may simply let the players have whatever they want and make them deal with subsequent cyberware damage. (There are a hundred ways to skin a chromed rat.)

CYBERWARE QUALITY

As veteran **Shadowrun** players and gamemasters already know, cyberware comes in various forms: standard, second-hand, alpha-grade, beta-grade, and even delta-grade. Alpha, beta, and delta grades represent various levels of quality and sophistication beyond standard, off-the-shelf cyberware. If alpha-grade cyberware is comparable to a simple home stereo system, delta-grade would represent a custom audiophile rack system. Both play music, but delta-grade is far more capable and reliable than alpha-grade. Second-hand cyberware comes in standard, alpha, and beta grades, but is less reliable than new cyberware of the same grade.

Only standard and alpha-grade cyberware are mass-produced. Beta-grade pieces are usually custom-made. Delta-grade cyberware is always custom-made for the individual, which makes it Essence-friendly but also prohibitively expensive. Medical costs and repair times for delta-grade cyberware are quadruple those for standard equipment. Essence reductions, cost multipliers, and damage resistance statistics for alpha, beta, and delta-grade cyberware appear below.

Player characters can get alpha- and beta-grade custom cyberware at most shadow clinics, but delta-grade cyberware is far more difficult to acquire. Stumbling across a delta-grade cyberware clinic is nearly impossible for Joe Shadowrunner. Some corps run such clinics, but a player character cannot just make an appointment to go in for a lube job. The corp has to *want* the character to be at the clinic (and if the corp wants someone, there's got to be a reason).

Some types of cyberware, especially anything involving cybermancy, require a delta-grade clinic for installation. For more information, see **Cybermancy**, pp. beginning on p. 64.

	Essence Reduction	Cost Multiplier	Damage Resistance
Alpha-grade	–20% (x .8)	x 3	5/6
Beta-grade	–40% (x .6)	x 7	4/5
Delta-grade	–50% (x .5)	x 10	3/4

ESSENCE REDUCTION

Reduce the amount of Base Essence Cost by the percentage listed (or use the multiplier given in parentheses). Round all numbers up. Essence Cost may never be reduced below .05 in this manner.

COST MULTIPLIER AND MEDICAL FEES

Multiply the cost for the cyberware by the number indicated. This represents *only* the cost for the piece of cyberware and does not include doctor's fees and hospitalization. For alpha- and beta-grade cybersurgery, doctor's fees and hospitalization are 50 times the rates listed on p. 145 of the Shadowrun basic rules. For delta-grade cybersurgery, the fees are 200 times the rates listed.

DAMAGE RESISTANCE

The first number given is the target for resisting damage from Serious Wounds, the second from Deadly Wounds. When a piece of custom cyberware is damaged, roll 5 dice against the target number indicated above. If a single success is achieved, the cyberware takes no damage.

GENERAL RULES ON DAMAGE

Rules for damage to cyberware previously published in The **Street Samurai Catalog** and **Shadowtech** deal with gross effects of damage and the procedures necessary for repairs. However, damage to cyberware can also cause extremely inconvenient secondary effects. For example, damaged cybereyes may begin to short out, suffer color shifts, and so on. Rules for the various kinds of cyberware addressed in this section include specific secondary effects of damage that gamemasters can use to bring a little spice and stress into the player characters' lives.

As an alternative to the rules in previous sourcebooks for determining whether and where cyberware damage occurs, gamemasters can use the following quick-and-dirty system. Whenever a character takes a Serious or Deadly Wound, the gamemaster rolls 2D6 after all Damage Resistance Tests are resolved. If the result is less than the number of boxes of damage taken (6 for Serious and 10 for Deadly), the character's cyberware takes damage. Because the possible combinations of cyberware that a player character may cram into his body are virtually infinite, the gamemaster decides what specific piece of cyberware has been damaged. The damage should have a logical connection with the location of the wound, and the gamemaster's choice should not unduly hinder the player character. The goal is to add more challenge to the game, but not make it impossible for player characters to succeed.

HEADWARE

The following rules apply to various types of headware, from communications gear to cybereyes and cyberears and their accessories.

COMMUNICATIONS

Information and basic rules for the headware radio and telephone appear on pp. 246–247, **SRII**. Those for the communications link, crypto-circuit HD, and scramble breaker HD appear in the **Street Samurai Catalog**, pp. 76, 77, and 81. Rules and information for the tactical communications system appear in **Fields of Fire**, pp. 59 and 86.

The cybercomm link is essentially a transducer that converts thoughts into speech, making it possible to communicate without talking aloud. Because the transducer has no transmitting or receiving capacity, using it as part of a communications system requires a radio transmitter. In addition to being useful for the clandestine communications of shadowrunners, the cybercomm link has revolutionized the lives of people who suffer from congenital muteness or have suffered severe damage to their vocal chords.

Jamming, Counter-Jamming and Encryption

Jamming and counter-jamming are achieved with ECM/ECCM add-ons to communication equipment (see **Using Equipment**, p. 184, **SRII**). To resolve jamming or counter-jamming attempts, make an opposed test pitting the rating of the jamming component against the rating of the counter-jamming component (or vice-versa). Characters who have a Special Skill related to the use of the jamming or counter-jamming element in question, or who have encephalon (see p. 49, **Shadowtech**), may add a number of additional dice up to the rating of the ECM/ECCM gear. The jammer or counter-jammer that achieves the greater number of net successes accomplishes its task; in the case of a tie, the jamming unit is successful. The number of net successes determines the overall success of the jamming or counter-jamming attempt. Multiply the number of success-

COMMUNICATIONS HEADWARE SECONDARY DAMAGE

Dice Roll Result	Secondary Effect
2–4	No effect, lucky you.
5–7	Static; garbles message.
8–9	Intermittent signal; approximately half of message gets through.
10–11	Unit functions intermittently and must be struck or jostled to work again after failure. For attempts to get it working, make a Quickness (3) Test.
12	Total unit failure; nothing but continual annoying static.

es by 10. The result is the percent of the message that is received or is blocked.

To resolve attempts at encryption and decryption of communications signals, use the same procedure as for jamming and counter-jamming.

Secondary Damage

If a headware communications unit takes damage, roll 2D6 and consult the Communications Headware Secondary Damage table to determine secondary effects.

All secondary effects continue until the damaged unit is repaired. If the gamemaster is using the quick-and-dirty damage system, the target number of any appropriate Repair Test is equal to one-half (round down) the secondary-effect dice roll result.

CYBEREYES AND ACCESSORIES

In general, any combination of accessories can be installed in a cybereye, subject to the following Essence limits. Per pair, cybereyes cost a player character .2 points of Essence on installation. The eyes can handle an additional .5 Essence points' worth of accessories, such as low-light amplification, without additional cost to the character. In other words, a total of .7 Essence points actually costs the character .2 Essence points. Cybereye accessories can be added or removed without impacting the Essence of the character. When dealing with beta- and delta-grade cybereyes, make the necessary adjustments for Essence loss before considering the .5 allowance for accessories.

Though cybereyes are usually purchased in pairs, they can be purchased singly. A single cybereye costs 60 percent of the standard purchase price, takes up .1 Essence and accepts accessories worth only .25 points of Essence before adding to the total Essence cost. Cybereye accessories that require a pair to work well, such as low-light amplification, thermographics, and cyberoptic camera or Smartcam systems (see pp. 89-90, **Shadowbeat**) are less effective in a single eye. The gamemaster may find it necessary to determine the exact loss of efficiency, but in general such systems operate about half as well in one eye as in two. Many other systems, such as a laser designator or a display link, are single-eye enhancements to begin with and so are not affected. Vision magnification systems can provide proper magnification with only one eye; however, they cannot provide any depth perception to characters with only one cybereye. A +4 modifier applies to the target number of any Combat Tests made while the vision magnification is active; this modifier is cumulative with other modifiers (if any). Needless to say, eye weapons and laser systems can only be mounted in a cybereye.

The small size of the (meta)human eye socket represents a built-in limitation to the number of accessories that can be installed in a cybereye. Player characters cannot walk around with guns, darts, lasers, cameras, and all kinds of other things packed into such a confined space. To reflect this, gamemasters should seriously consider the following limits. Accessories worth a maximum of 1.2 Essence points can be installed in a pair of cybereyes (including the free .5 Essence points conferred by the standard rules), and only one accessory per eye may be a weapon system. Player characters hoping to get around that limitation by installing a tool laser that can function as an extra weapon are out of luck; a single cybereye cannot mount a tool laser and a gun or dart. In addition, a cybereye with a cybercam installed in it cannot accomodate a weapon system or a tool laser because there is not sufficient room. (Of course, there's

CYBEREYE SECONDARY DAMAGE

Dice Roll Result	Secondary Effect
2–4	No effect, lucky you.
5–6	Black-and-white image.
7	Blurred vision; add +2 to all target numbers for tests involving perception at a distance.
8–9	Image intermittent; eye must be struck or jostled to work again after failure. To get it working, make a Quickness (3) Test.
10–11	One eye fails; add a +4 modifier to the target number for any tests involving depth perception.
12	Total unit failure; signal provides nothing but continual annoying static.

nothing to stop the really determined from installing a different weapon in each eye.)

Secondary Damage

If a cybereye takes damage, roll 2D6 and consult the Cybereye Secondary Damage table to determine secondary effects. A character who uses an eye gun automatically damages his cybereyes because of the shock of recoil in such a confined space. Even with the stabilization systems available, recoil in the orbital cavity remains an almost insoluble problem. Eye guns should be treated as one-shot items for desperate situations.

All secondary effects continue until the unit is repaired. If the gamemaster is using the quick-and-dirty damage system, the target number of any appropriate Repair Tests is equal to one-half (round down) the secondary-effect dice roll result.

Eye Dataports and Optical Scanning Datajacks

The standard data flow rate (DFR) of an eye dataport is 25 (the DFR of the standard datajack in **SRII**). To find costs for ports with higher DFRs, add .05 to the Essence Cost and double the purchase price listed below for each 25-point increase to the DFR (to a maximum of 100).

Level	DFR	Essence Cost	Price
1	25	.10	500¥
2	50	.15	1,000¥
3	75	.20	2,000¥
4	100	.25	4,000¥

For an optical scanning datajack, the standard DFR is 20. To find costs for optical datajacks with higher DFRs, use the rules given above for eye dataports. Note that the cost increase applies to the emitter as well.

The description of the optical scanning datajack (**Comfortably Numb**, p. 20) refers to "pressing on the iris" to render the datajack functional. Literally pressing on the iris would temporarily blind that eye. To keep this from occurring, optical scanning datajacks are either mounted in a secondary iris-like structure not apparent to casual inspection, or they feature a mirror to refract light to the cyber-retina.

BrightLight Systems

The reusable BrightLight flash system operates like the standard flash-pak (**Street Samurai Catalog**, p. 45). Opponents facing the light system receive a +4 modifier to their target numbers for all ranged attacks; flare compensation reduces this modifier to +2. In addition, the target number modifier is reduced by 1 for every 5 meters that the opponent is standing from the character using the eye light system. The system also negates the effects of poor or absent lighting for the duration of its use, but the strobe effect imposes a +2 modifier to all the user's target numbers.

The flash-pak unit can flash three times before the battery must be replaced. A replacement battery costs 150¥ and takes 10 minutes to install.

The battery and bulb for the high-powered one-shot flash-pak must be replaced after every use. Replacement batteries and bulbs are commonly available at a cost of 10¥ each. The batteries can also be bought in packs of six for 50¥. The flash only affects targets directly in front of the user. If a question arises as to whether or not the target is looking directly at the user, the gamemaster may (at his discretion) resolve the dispute with an opposed test pitting the Reaction of the user against the Reaction of the target. The target's net successes apply to his Damage Resistance Test. The user's net successes do not apply, as the game mechanic already assumes that the target is looking the user full in the face.

The nature of this weapon precludes the need for a Combat Test. Instead, each target must make a Damage Resistance Test against a target number equal to 12 minus the number of meters away from the user they are standing. The BrightLight system does Serious Stun damage, and the target must also apply a modifier to the target numbers for all visual tests equal to the number of boxes of damage done. This effect fades at the rate of 1 point per minute. If the target suffers a Deadly Wound, certain effects may become permanent at the gamemaster's discretion.

The BrightLight flash is visible for three kilometers, unless line of sight is somehow blocked. Used inside a building or room, the light will seep through any crack or opening and might even be visible throughout an entire floor. Users also risk blinding friends as well as foes. To determine whether or not this happens, the gamemaster should apply a version of the **Blast in a Confined Space** rules (p. 97, **SRII**), assuming a starting Power Level of 12 that degrades by 1 for every meter that the light travels. Under this rule, even someone standing behind the user might be blinded by the flash. Also, whenever a character uses the BrightLight flash, the gamemaster rolls 2D6. On a result of 2 or 3, the user is blinded and must replace his cybereyes.

Eye Laser Systems

Eye lasers and light systems run on battery power, which means that player characters who have them must carry the batteries (and a couple of spares, if they're smart) somewhere. Batteries supplying power to such systems can be stored anywhere on the character's person. A character can even carry laser batteries externally, connecting them to the laser system via an interface so that he can change power packs when needed without having to open up interesting body cavities that a runner might not want exposed in dangerous situations. The gamemaster determines how runners equipped with these systems can manage to plug in and recharge. However, it is unlikely that the need for such details will arise often in game play. Eye lasers have extremely specific uses, and should not become major elements of any character's personal arsenal.

CYBEREAR ACCESSORIES

At the gamemaster's discretion, special rules may apply when using the spatial recognizer in certain situations—for example, when attempting to locate something or someone moving around a corner or in a maze of corridors. In such cases, the gamemaster may appply a –1 modifier to the target numbers of all Perception Tests made to locate an object or person. This modifier only applies in visually dull environments—featureless corporate corridors, boringly decorated interiors painted in drab colors,

CYBEREAR SECONDARY DAMAGE

Dice Roll Result	Secondary Effect
2-4	No effect, lucky you.
5-6	Lower end of the sound spectrum cuts out.
7	Static; add a +2 modifier to all target numbers for tests to discern sounds.
8-9	Sound intermittent; ear must be struck or jostled to work again after failure. To get it working, make a Quickness (3) Test.
10-11	One ear fails. Apply a +4 modifier to the target number for all tests involving spatial sound perception.
12	Total unit failure; user hears nothing except continual, annoying static.

and so on. The spatial recognizer is most effective when visual input is absent or restricted, because visual input tends to be dominant when the brain processes information. Therefore, an overabundance of things to look at swamps the spatial recognizer and renders it virtually useless.

Secondary Damage

If a cyberear takes damage, roll 2D6 and consult the Cyberear Secondary Damage table to determine the secondary effects.

All secondary effects continue until the unit is repaired. If the gamemaster is using the quick-and-dirty damage system, the target number of all appropriate Repair Tests is equal to one-half (round down) the secondary effect dice roll result.

ORAL WEAPONS

Oral darts and guns are usually concealed in a compartment in the roof of the mouth. When triggered, they drop into shooting position and fire when the character opens his mouth. The gamemaster may impose penalties on characters equipped with oral darts or guns when such characters make Perception Tests using their innate sense of smell, because such cyberware may interfere with sinus functioning.

The oral spur and whip are becoming popular among certain hardcore street samurai because they are significantly less common and harder to spot than such weapons as hand razors. Some rough-edged bullyboys believe that the unexpectedness of these oral weapons gives them an edge in combat. Also, a character can use these weapons even when his hands and legs are tied. In general, however, the limitations on oral weapons (small number of shots and/or short ranges) make them useful only in highly specialized situations.

The oral whip can only be used effectively if the character can impart momentum from head movement. Though the whip is powered, it tends to pop out like an extra-strong party streamer if the user's head is restrained or still. The gamemaster may decide to reduce the whip's Damage Code if a character uses this weapon while his head is restrained. A control mechanism monitors the user's head position at all times to ensure that the whip always retracts smoothly and does not strike the user inadvertently.

CRANIAL BOMBS

The common name, "cortex bomb," is actually something of a misnomer. The microbomb has a devastating effect if placed near any major internal organ—close to the heart, for example, or next to a major spinal nerve group. The area bomb kills no matter where it is located in a person's body. The term "cortex bomb" is historical in origin; initially these deadly devices were located in the central nervous system to make their surgical removal extremely difficult. In those long-departed days of the 2020's, brain surgery was a more chancy business than it is in 2055. Corporations who placed these bombs in their couriers liked being able to activate the bombs and dispose of compromised couriers before the opposition could get at the information they wanted. Cortex bombs also made useful devices for blackmail and coercion.

Although they are most often placed in the brain, kink bombs can be implanted near any expensive piece of cyberware. They are often implanted in cyberlimbs. Cyberlimbs are expensive, and few people will risk losing them by disobeying orders.

The gamemaster may adjust the cost of area bombs with different Damage Codes, but should consider a minimum of 300,000¥ for the weakest versions.

BODYWARE

The following rules apply to various types of bodyware, from dermal plating and sheaths to cyberlimbs.

DERMAL PLATING

Repairing damage done to dermal plating by a Serious or Deadly Wound requires a spray bonder that re-bonds the damaged dermal fiber weave by augmenting the fiber's innate self-repairing properties. A repair kit with this spray bonder costs 500¥ for 10 applications. Failure to use the spray bonder may result in long-term damage to the weave. If a player character with dermal plating takes damage to it from a Serious or Deadly Wound and does not use the spray bonder on the damaged plating within 24 hours, the gamemaster should note that fact. From then on, whenever that character suffers a Serious or Deadly Wound (after resolution of the Damage Resistance Test) from non-explosive weapons or magic, the gamemaster rolls 2D6. If the

result is less than the number of times the character has failed to use the spray bonder on a damaged area, the effective rating of the dermal plating is reduced by 1. The character must check his plating every time he suffers a Serious or Deadly Wound, and the reductions are cumulative.

A street doc can repair this damage—for a price. To repair 1 point of the plating's protection, a street doc normally charges 2,000¥ multiplied by the total number of points that the plating has lost. For example, a character whose dermal plating has been reduced by 2 points would be charged 4,000¥ to repair the first point (2,000¥ x 2) and another 2,000¥ to repair the second (2,000¥ x 1). The player character can modify this fee by making a standard Negotiation Test; each net success the character achieves lowers the final price by 5 percent. The actual work requires a biotech shop and a Biotech (5) Test with a Base Time of 4 hours per point. Technically, characters with the necessary skills and access to the necessary hardware can attempt these repairs on their own; the raw materials cost 400¥, multiplied by twice the number of points being repaired.

As stated in **Comfortably Numb** (p. 28), skin near dermal plating tends to heal poorly in the area of Serious or Deadly Wounds. Runners who wish to avoid scarring can buy a healing lotion that costs 20¥ per tube for 30 applications. For more information, see **Scarring**, p. 56.

DERMAL SHEATHING

Though similar in many ways to dermal plating, dermal sheathing is easier to care for and repair, though repairs are more expensive. Only a Deadly Wound can cause a permanent reduction in the rating of dermal sheathing. The base cost of repairs is 6,500¥ per point (1,400¥ raw materials cost); the work requires a Biotech (4) Test and takes a Base Time of 5 hours.

As long as the semi-artificial skin is sprayed with a chemical sealer within 12 hours of damage, there will be no scarring. The sealer spray costs 1,200¥ for 10 applications. If the damaged sheathing is not sprayed, Minor scarring occurs (see **Scarring,** p. 56).

A character cannot gain the benefits of both dermal plating and dermal sheathing. Sheathing is a superior form of plating and can only be fitted if pre-existing plating over the same area is removed. Note that orthoskin (p. 17, **Shadowtech**) is not compatible with dermal sheathing.

CYBERLIMB SECONDARY DAMAGE

Dice Roll Result	Secondary Effect
2–4	No effect, lucky you.
5–7	The limb twitches at random. Add a +1 modifier to target numbers for all tests using that limb.
8–9	On a 2D6 roll with a result of 10 or greater, the limb does not perform properly. The specific effect is up to the gamemaster.
10–11	On a 2D6 roll with a result of 8 or greater, the limb fails to perform properly.
12	The limb shuts down completely, except for an occasional twitch.

ARMOR

As stated in **Comfortably Numb**, armor can be acquired for cyberlimbs, torsos and skulls. **Shadowrun** does not use a hit location system, and so player characters who want full protection must acquire armor for each of five possible hit locations: arms, legs, head, front of torso, and back of torso. To find the overall Armor Rating, add up the ratings of the individual pieces of armor and average the result, rounding down. For example, the hotshot street samurai Razor's Edge has 4 points of armor on his chest, 2 points covering his back, 2 points covering his legs, 2 points on his arms, and 1 point protecting his head. This gives him a total of 11 points of armor plating distributed around his body (4 + 2 + 2 + 2 + 1 = 11). To find the average, divide the sum (11) by 5 (total possible hit locations). The result is 2.2,rounded down to 2, and so Razor's Edge has an overall Ballistic and Impact Armor Rating of 2. To keep players from doing such senseless things as putting all 10 points of armor in a cyberskull, the gamemaster may decree that any rating higher than 4 in any one area does not count for purposes of determining the overall Armor Rating. This limitation should ensure a sensible distribution of armor.

GENERAL RULES FOR CYBERLIMBS

Though simple replacement limbs with no special capabilities do exist in the world of **Shadowrun** (p. 249, **SRII**), most (if not all) shadowrunners who acquire cyberlimbs will buy the obviously cybernetic kind that can be modified and enhanced. The following rules apply to the latter type of cyberarm.

Pairs of cyberlimbs act as a layer of dermal plating, adding +1 to the character's Body. A character with a pair of cyberarms and a pair of cyberlegs adds +2 to his Body. Partial limbs, hands, and feet do not add to a character's Body.

Cyberhands and feet retain all the flexibility of their natural counterparts; in fact, they tend to move more fluidly than real hands or feet. A single cyberhand or foot adds +1 to the Power of unarmed combat attacks; any two cyberhands or feet (two hands, two feet, or one of each) adds +2 to the Power of unarmed combat attacks. More than two cyberhands or feet confer no additional bonus.

Detecting Cyberlimbs

The base target number for detecting an undisguised cyberlimb is 4, assuming a reasonably short period of interaction. If, for example, someone spends an entire evening at a bar in the company of a character with a cyberlimb, that base target number is reduced by a minimum –2 modifier. This modifier may drop as low as –4 at the gamemaster's discretion, depending on such factors as the duration, frequency, and continuity of observation. Cyberlimbs never move quite as naturally as the real thing, and after awhile the onlooker will notice. A cyberlimb becomes even more obvious if a character is drunk; the artificial limb does not flail around with quite the right degree of abandon.

Secondary Damage

If a cyberlimb takes damage, roll 2D6 and consult the Cyberlimb Secondary Damage table to determine secondary effects.

Cyberware-Cyberlimb Compatibility

When certain pieces of cyberware are wired into a cyberlimb, the limb reduces or eliminates the cyberware's Essence Cost. The Cyberware-Cyberlimb Compatibility table indicates the adjusted Essence Cost for the specific pieces to which this rule applies. In most cases, the Essence Cost of cyberware comes from the neural interface and secondary connections that allow control of the cyberware in question, and so the presence of a cyberlimb does not adjust Essence Cost.

CYBERWARE-CYBERLIMB COMPATIBILITY

	Adjusted Essence Cost
Fingertip Compartment	0
Spurs and Razors (all kinds)	0
Smartgun Links (all kinds)	.25
Tactical Computer	–25% (round down)
Orientation System	.25

Cyberlimbs and Bone Lacing

Bone lacing (p. 42, **Shadowtech**) cannot be performed on cyberlimbs. The armor value for bone lacing does not apply to cyberlimbs, though it does apply to a character's residual meat body. As a rule of thumb, characters can have two complete cyber replacements without losing bonuses for previously applied bone lacing. For characters with three cyber replacements, subtract 1 from bone lacing armor bonuses; for more than 3 replacements, all such bonuses are lost. (A single limb—such as the right arm or left leg—counts as one replacement for these purposes. Skulls and torsos count as single replacement as well.)

STRENGTH ENHANCEMENTS

The following rules for Strength enhancements offer a new level of complexity, and so gamemasters and players alike should study them carefully before using them.

All cyberlimbs are assumed to have a built-in Strength of 3. If characters choose to enhance their cyberlimbs—or beef up their natural limbs with muscle replacement and/or augmentation—they may have to deal with problems that can surface when different limbs end up with different Strength ratings. (Imagine a character whose left arm has Strength 3, right arm Strength 5, a right leg Strength 7, and a left leg Strength 4. Yikes!)

If a character's various limbs have different Strength ratings, the true rating of any given limb can only be used in specific circumstances. The gamemaster must determine what happens in any given situation, as the possibilities are too numerous to devise rules for in detail. As a broad guideline, assume that if the character can apply a particular limb properly in a given situation, that limb's full Strength Rating can be used. For example, a character trying to pull up someone who has fallen over the edge of a building can use the true Strength Rating for the limb that is actually supporting the fallen person. In this same situation, the character cannot use the Strength Ratings of his other limbs unless he manages to get leverage or bracing that allows the application of strength from them. If a character manages to apply more than one limb in a given situation, use the average of all the Strength Ratings (round down) for those limbs.

In certain situations, such as unarmed or armed combat, it is impossible to tell for certain when and how a particular limb is being used. In this case, the player must choose between one or the other of the following alternatives.

The player's character may use an average Strength Rating—adding up the Strength ratings of all four limbs and then dividing by four (rounding down)—as the Strength Rating for melee combat. If the character also has muscle replacement or muscle augmentation, the appropriate Strength bonuses apply to all limbs equally and should be added to the Strength of each natural limb.

Alternatively, the player can have his character try to lead with the highest-strength limb the character possesses. This option allows a character to take full advantage of enhanced limbs.

A player who makes this choice finds the average Strength Rating mentioned above and must apply a modifier to the target numbers for Melee Combat Tests equal to the difference between that average and the Strength Rating of the chosen limb. For example, a character with one arm at Strength 3, the other at Strength 5, a right leg at Strength 4 and a left leg at Strength 7 has an average Strength Rating 4. If this character wants to lead with his Strength 5 arm, he must fight with a +1 modifier to the target number for all Melee Combat Tests (5 – 4 = 1).

Limitations

Any single cyberlimb can only handle a maximum of 3 points of Strength enhancement before additional Essence and nuyen must be spent to modify the body to handle the extra stress. Each point of strength enhancement beyond 3 requires an additional .4 points of Essence and another 25,000¥. A character having his arm enhanced must undergo cybersurgery for the mounting reinforcement on the shoulder or elbow, depending on whether the character has a full cyberarm or a partial one. Enhancements to legs require cybersurgery on the hip for a full limb and the knee for a partial.

A character may possess an average augmented Strength Rating up to a maximum of twice his Body, or Body + 4, whichever is lower. A character with Body 3 can have an average Strength Rating no greater than 6; a troll character with Body 9 can have an average Strength no greater than 13.

Partial Cyberlimbs

Characters may boost the inherent strength of cyberhands and feet, but the boosted strength does not add to the Power of unarmed combat attacks. Such enhancements cost 65,000¥ per point of additional hand or foot strength to a maximum of +3 and cost no additional Essence. Increased hand strength can only be applied to gripping, not arm leverage.

Cyber lower arms and legs work like cyberhands and feet, except that strength enhancements for them cost 120,000¥ per point—60,000¥ if the adjacent hand or foot already has enhanced strength.

Trolls and Cyberlimbs

Strength enhancements for cyberlimbs apply differently to troll characters than to characters of other races. For non-troll characters, their relatively low Strength makes the hefty Essence losses for large Strength enhancements (+4 and up) of cyberlimbs reasonable—these characters are getting far more than their basic biology allows them to accomodate, and the invasive work needed to support the limb should entail big-time Essence loss. Trolls, by contrast, have an average Strength of 8. Under normal rules, a troll whose arm got ripped off would have to pay 2 Essence points to get a cyberarm that matched his average biological strength, with no bonuses at all. To compensate for this unfair penalty, treat the basic Strength of a cyberlimb for a troll as 8 instead of the usual 3. Cyberlimbs with Strength enhancements higher than 8 cost troll characters the standard .4 Essence loss per point.

QUICKNESS ENHANCEMENTS

Quickness enhancements to cyberlimbs must be balanced across a pair of limbs. A pair of cyberarms or a pair of cyberlegs must have the same level of Quickness enhancements. If they do not, the player character must apply a modifier equal to the difference between the limbs' Quickness Ratings to the target numbers for all tests involving movement or coordination of any kind. Modifiers from arm and leg pairs are cumulative.

Determine the average Quickness of multiple enhanced limbs as for Strength enhancements. Quickness altered in this manner affects Reaction and Initiative.

Limitations

As with Strength enhancements, any single cyberlimb can only handle a maximum of 3 points of Quickness enhancement before a player character must spend additional Essence and nuyen to modify the body to handle the extra stress. Each point of Quickness enhancement beyond 3 requires an additional .3 points of Essence and another 20,000¥. Cybersurgery is required for additional mounting reinforcement to the appropriate joint.

The maximum average enhanced Quickness a character can possess is equal to twice his natural Quickness (including any bioware the character may have) or Quickness + 4, whichever is lower. For example, a character with Quickness 3 can have an average enhanced Quickness Rating of no greater than 6; an elf character with Quickness 9 can have an average enhanced Quickness no greater than 13.

BODY ENHANCEMENTS

Body enhancements give a character protection above and beyond the equivalent layer of dermal armor received for each pair of cyberarms or legs. Body enhancements can only be applied to pairs of limbs, up to a maximum of an additional +3 Body per pair. A character with a pair of cyberarms and full Body enhancements would receive +3 to his Body Rating. If the character has cyberarms and cyberlegs with full Body enhancements, his Body Rating rises by +6.

Body enhancements cost no additional Essence. However, they bulk up a limb significantly, making it much more difficult to conceal its nature. For each point of Body Enhancement per pair of cyberlimbs, apply a –1 modifier to the target numbers of any visual Perception Tests made to notice and recognize cyberlimbs (see **Perception,** p. 185, **SRII**; also **Detecting Cyberlimbs**, p. 49).

MULTIPLE ENHANCEMENTS

Players who choose to give their characters multiple types of enhancements to the same limb will discover that the requirements and modifications for one type of enhancement are often at odds with those of another. To reflect this fact, add 10 percent to the purchase price of any additional enhancements. For example, a character who already has a Strength enhancement in one cyberarm must pay an additional 10 percent of the cost of Quickness or Body enhancements he wants to add. If the character adds Quickness and later adds Body, he must pay an extra 10 percent of the cost of the Quickness enhancement and 10 percent of the cost of the Body enhancement. If he wishes to add Quickness and Body enhancements at the same time, the costs for both increase by 10 percent.

DANGLING AND HOLDING

The introduction of the cyberlimb magnetic system begs the question of just how long a character can dangle, lift, and hold on in various situations. The character's weight, the weight of any object the character may be holding on to, and the character's Strength, Body and Willpower ratings may all come into play, depending on the specific action the character is trying to accomplish. Keep in mind that the following game mechanics do not accurately reflect all the possibilities in real-life situations. To spell out rules in such detail would require complex geometric progressions that only a mathematician could love. These rules are intended as rough guidelines to keep things simple, and gamemasters may modify them as they see fit.

A character's weight is determined by his Body Rating. Different races have different ratios of weight to Body points, as indicated by the racial averages listed on the table on p. 52. To determine a character's approximate weight, consult the Weight to Body Table and multiply the listed kilograms by the character's Body Rating.

WEIGHT TO BODY TABLE

Race	Kilograms per point of Body
Dwarf	13
Elf/Human	24
Ork	16
Troll	28

Though actual weight may vary from character to character, using the Weight to Body Table allows the gamemaster to make a rough approximation. The weight-to-Body ratio also applies to increases in Body conferred by cyberware.

For each point of Strength a character with one cyberarm possesses, he can hold 15 kilograms with that arm. A character with two cyberarms can hold a total of 30 kilograms for each point of Strength. However, the character can only hold that weight without difficulty for a time period equal to the sum of his Strength, Body, and Willpower ratings, multiplied by 15 seconds. For example, an average human (Strength 3, Body 3, Willpower 3) can hold up to 45 kilograms (Strength 3 x 15 kilograms) for a base time of two minutes and fifteen seconds (9 x 15 seconds = 135 seconds, or 2 min. 15 sec.).

For every 5 kilograms or part thereof that the weight exceeds the character's limit, the base time is reduced by 20 percent (round up). For example, assume that an average human is trying to hold on to something that weighs 70 kilograms. The object in question is 25 kilograms over the character's weight limit (70 – 45 = 25), which means that the 20-percent reduction in the base holding time applies five times—once for every five extra kilograms (25 divided by 5 = 5). Twenty times 5 equals 100, and so the base holding time is reduced by 100 percent. This character has to struggle to hold on to the object right away.

If a character is holding something that weighs less than the maximum he can hang on to, the holding time rises by 10 percent (rounding up) for every 5 kilograms or portion thereof below the character's limit. For example, an average human is holding on to an object that weighs 30 kilograms, or 15 kilograms below that character's limit (45 – 30 = 15). The 10-percent increase in the base holding time applies three times (15 divided by 5 = 3), for a total increase of 30 percent. Thirty percent of 135 seconds equals 40.5 seconds; added to the base holding time of 2 minutes and 15 seconds, this means that the character can hold the object without difficulty for just under 3 minutes (2 minutes and 56 seconds).

Once a character reaches his limit, he must make a test pitting the sum of his Strength and Willpower ratings against a target number equal to the weight of the object being held divided by 15 (rounding up). For example, an average human holding on to a 45-kilogram load rolls 6 dice (Strength 3 + Willpower 3 = 6) against a Target Number 3 (45 kg divided by 15 = 3). If the test fails, the character drops the object. If the test is successful, the character holds on to the object for another 2 Combat Rounds (6 seconds). In the third Combat Round the character must make another test, with a +1 modifier to the target number. An additional +1 modifier applies to every subsequent test made to continue hanging on to the object.

Once the character reaches his limit he must also begin making Damage Resistance Tests against a Power Rating equal to the amount of weight he is attempting to hold, divided by 15 (rounding up). For example, an average human holding on to a 45-kilogram weight would make a Damage Resistance Test against a Target Number 3 (45 divided by 15 = 3). An average human attempting to hold 75 kilograms would make a Damage Resistance Test against a Target Number 5 (75 divided by 15 = 5).

Attempts to hold heavy objects cause Light Stun damage at first. The damage increases by one level for each multiple or part thereof of the base weight the character can hold, rounding up. Damage is taken immediately. An average human holding onto a 45-kilogram weight would make his Damage Resistance Test for Light Stun damage; the same character attempting to hold a 75-kilogram weight would make a Damage Resistance Test for Moderate Stun damage.

If a character attempts to hold on to an object that weighs less than 20 percent of the maximum, he can hold the object indefinitely. Excessively heavy weights are up to the gamemaster to decide. Player characters should get at least some chance to pull off the heroic, one-turn hanging-on act with something really heavy, but holding on to a rhino falling off a skyscraper is out of the question.

For dangling characters attempting to keep their grip on something, the character's weight functions as the maximum weight he can easily hold. When cumulative damage from the character's exertions renders the character unconscious, the character falls. If the gamemaster wishes, he may make a Willpower (6) Test for the character once the cumulative damage reaches the Deadly level. Success allows the character to hang on for a period of time determined by the gamemaster. If no successes are achieved, the character loses his grip and plummets. Keep in mind, however, that imposing this option is somewhat harsh for a character in such a life-or-death situation.

CYBERGUNS

Cyberguns mounted in a cyberlimb cost no Essence. Cyberguns mounted in a natural limb or other body part do cost Essence, as indicated on the Cybergun Essence Costs table.

Additional rules for cyberguns appear on p. 86, **Street Samurai Catalog, Second Edition**.

CYBERGUN ESSENCE COSTS

Weapon	Essence Cost
Hold-out Pistol	.15
Light Pistol	.35
Machine Pistol	.4
Submachine Gun	.6
Heavy Pistol	1
Shotgun	1.1

CYBERARM GYROMOUNT

The effective Strength employed for the purposes of recoil modifiers (p. 83, **Fields of Fire**) is the Strength of the cyberarm in which the gyromount is located, not the Strength of the character's meat body.

CYBERSURGERY

Cybersurgery requires a skill test on the part of the performing surgeon. The surgeon may use the Biotech (B/R) Skill or one of its appropriate Concentrations or Specializations, or an appropriate Special Skill at the discretion of the gamemaster. The base target number for this skill test is equal to 10 minus the Essence that the character intends to end up with (rounding down). For example, if a character is having cyberware installed that would result in an Essence of 2.3, the Base Target Number would be 8 (10 – 2 = 8).

Appropriate modifiers to the skill test target number appear in the Doctoring Table (p. 113, **SRII**). The character is assumed to be in Intensive Care but may or may not have access to long-term magical care at the discretion of the gamemaster. Note, however, that alpha-, beta-, and delta-grade clinics always have healing magicians on staff. All other modifiers apply as needed.

These rules assume that the surgery is successful—medical science in 2056 has progressed to a point where table deaths are rare. The skill test determines exactly how well the cyber-implant surgery was performed, especially the delicate work of the neurological interface. The successes achieved by the doctor can raise or lower the actual Essence Cost of the cyberware being installed, as indicated on the Essence Cost Change Table.

Apply the percentage indicated to the Essence Cost of the piece of cyberware, rounding up. If the result would leave the character with less than 0 Essence, assume the surgery is aborted. The character survives, but with an Essence Rating of 0. If the character in question is at a delta clinic, cybermancy is an option (see **Cybermancy**, p. 64).

The gamemaster may choose not to reveal to the player his character's actual Essence Rating. Instead, the gamemaster may simply state what it rounds to for the purposes of magical healing. The character must then decide whether to risk additional cybersurgery at a later date.

Note that cybersurgery is elective surgery (pp. 114–115, **SRII**). In addition to the in-hospital healing time costs, the actual surgery also costs nuyen, as indicated on the following table.

ESSENCE COST CHANGE TABLE

Successes	Essence Cost Change
None	+15%
1	+10%
2-3	no change
4-5	–10%
6 or more	–20%

MEDICAL COSTS TABLE

Wound Level	Cost (in nuyen)
First Aid	
Deadly	400
Serious	200
Moderate	100
Light	50
Doctor's Services	
Deadly	400 per day
Serious	200 per day
Moderate	100 per day
Light	50 per day
Hospitalization	
Lifestyle (includes doctor's services)	500 per day
Intensive Care	
(only if Hospitalization Lifestyle applies)	1,000 per day
Surgery (includes cost of surgeon)	
Minor Cosmetic	1,000
Minor Invasive	5,000
Major Invasive	25,000
Drastic Invasive	250,000
Body Parts (Base Time to Grow)	
Eye (6 weeks)	10,000
Limb (10 weeks)	30,000
Organ (6 weeks)	20,000
Forced Growth (maximum rating 10)	Cost x Rating
Divides time to grow by rating	
Reduces compatibility by rating	

EFFECTS OF WIRED REFLEXES

Characters with wired reflexes or any other kind of cybernetic reflex enhancements are prone to react without thinking, because they are constantly on edge. At the gamemaster's discretion, such a character tends to react reflexively in situations where a perceived threat exists, regardless of whether or not that threat is real. The unexpected appearance of a stranger or dangerous-looking people, a sudden threatening move or action, and a violent motion in a crowd are all things that might set off a wired character. In such situations, have the character make a Perception Test (p.185, **SRII**). Apply a +1 modifier to the target number per +1D6 Initiative bonus the character possesses. This modifier represents the character's tendency to react before fully analyzing the situation. However, the character may also make a Willpower Test against the unmodified target number for the Perception Test to see if he can hold off his (probably destructive) reaction.

The gamemaster should use this rule sparingly, as an occasional reminder of what it's like to live on the edge. Constantly subjecting the character to it will turn him into a hyperactive nervous wreck and won't be much fun for the player. Reserve this mental torture for appropriate situations—potentially threatening crowds, lonely dark streets, and particularly tense encounters.

EFFECTS OF MOVE-BY-WIRE SYSTEMS

This piece of cyberware can make a character lethal in combat, but it has drawbacks to match its advantages. Putting the central nervous system into a state of constant seizure, as this system does, risks precipitating some unpleasant side effects: TLE-x (Temporal Lobe Epilepsy with complications) and CCSS (Catastrophic Clonic Seizure Syndrome).

To check for TLE-x and CCSS, the gamemaster makes Attribute Tests at regular intervals for players whose characters have the move-by-wire system. The average of the character's Body and Willpower ratings determines the number of dice used for the test. Magical bonuses to Attributes do not apply to these tests; round fractions down. The maximum augmentation of a character's Body Rating from cyber enhancements is +2, as these enhancements have a limited capacity to affect the chances of the character's brain going AWOL. The frequency of the tests and the relevant target numbers depend on the level of move-by-wire system the character possesses, as shown on the Complication Test Table.

The gamemaster can make these tests at scheduled dates or after a character experiences excessive physical or emotional stress. The tests should be made when the character is unaffected by any spells that might temporarily boost relevant Attributes, as TLE-x or CCSS are more likely to occur when an individual has weakened resistance. If the gamemaster achieves 2 successes, the character avoids complications. One success means that the character has developed TLE-x. If no successes are achieved, the character has developed CCSS or both CCSS and TLE-x, at the gamemaster's discretion.

COMPLICATION TEST TABLE

Move-by-Wire Level	Test Frequency	Target Number
1	Every 6 months	3
2	Every 4 months	4
3	Every 4 months	5
4	Every 3 months	6

TLE-X

TLE-x is a condition loosely based on basic TLE syndrome. Feelings of alienation, depersonalization, and perceptual distortions characterize the condition. Coordination of perceptions and actions, and judging spatial relationships becomes difficult due to a secondary focus developing in the motor systems. In circumstances that the gamemaster deems dangerous or tactically crucial—such as whether an individual notices some clue or sign—a +2 penalty is applied to target numbers for Perception Tests, Initiative is reduced by 2, and Reaction is reduced by 1D6. The character also suffers a –1 penalty to Charisma and all Charisma-based skills in important social situations; the depersonalization and alienation make his social responses subtly inappropriate.

TLE-x can be treated by a physician who makes a successful Biotech/Transimplant Surgery (8) Test. However, this procedure cuts away a small area of brain tissue that has become chronically dysfunctional, and the guy in the white coat can only do this a limited number of times. A second occurrence of the syndrome can be treated with a successful Biotech/Transimplant Surgery (10) Test. After that the condition becomes chronic and cannot be corrected. In the case of chronic TLE-x, the epileptic foci can spread and the unfortunate victim can develop exciting and romantic afflictions like impotence and incontinence. The gamemaster may decrease Social skills and Charisma as he sees fit.

The individual with chronic TLE-x may also suffer acute seizures. If such a character suffers a Moderate (or worse) Wound and is engaged in combat or some other type of conflict, the player must make a Willpower (6) Test. If the test fails, the character collapses in an epileptic seizure and suffers 6M Damage. The individual becomes unconscious after 10 x 1D6 Combat Turns and remains out cold for 10 x 1D6 minutes.

CCSS

CCSS is a catastrophic breakdown of brain functions. Chronic seizures grip all major perceptual, motor and associative regions. Basic vegetative functions such as breathing work more or less normally, but the affected character is incapable of voluntary action and is barely aware of what is happening around him. He experiences the world as a terrifying, whirling chaos of nightmarish sensations and intense pain.

CCSS renders a victim's move-by-wire system permanently dysfunctional and it must be removed. If a character with CCSS cannot find a doctor to perform the necessary treatments, he must make a successful (Unaugmented) Body (5) Test every hour or the character dies. For characters who undergo treatment, long-term rehabilitation is required. Such rehabilitation must last (10 – Unaugmented Body) weeks, to a minimum of 5, and includes intensive care, corrective brain surgery enough drugs to sink the Titanic, and lots more (at a cost of 50,000¥ per week).

Of course, simply undergoing surgery and follow-up treatment is no guarantee that the character will be just fine. To determine possible long-term damage from CCSS, the treating physician makes a Biotech/Transimplant Surgery (10) Test. The CCSS Recovery Table indicates the effects of various roll results. If the physician achieves no successes, for example, the patient suffers Damage Level 4; his Strength, Quickness, and Willpower are all permanently reduced by 1, and his Intelligence level becomes 0—he lives, but with no more mind than a hairbrush. At least 1 success means the patient eventually returns to near normal functioning, although he suffers the permanent reductions in Attributes as shown on the table. Note these rules assume the best possible medical care; this work can only be performed in an intensive-care unit. Any attempt to perform this work outside such a facility fails automatically.

The implication of these rules for game play is that Level 1–3 move-by-wire systems may not pose too many hazards for people with big-time bods and/or steely wills. Level 4 systems are for those who want to live fast and

CCSS RECOVERY TABLE

Successes	Damage Level	Effects
6	1	–1 Quickness and Willpower
4	2	–1 Quickness, Intelligence, and Willpower
2	3	–1 Strength, Quickness, and Willpower; –2 Intelligence
0	4	–1 Strength, Quickness, and Willpower; Intelligence level 0 (you lucky lobotomy case, you). Adaptation to the social world is possible at the level of a family pet.

die horribly in the near future—or for truly appalling NPCs the sadistic gamemaster wants to unleash on runners.

SCARRING

For players who want to know when their characters get scars and how nasty they are, use the following guidelines. Whenever a character takes a Serious or Deadly Wound, have him make a Body Test against a target number equal to the number of boxes of damage taken. Apply the appropriate target number modifiers listed in the Scarring Modifiers Table.

SCARRING MODIFIERS TABLE

Treatment Conditions	Modifier
Intensive care (in hospital)	–4
Not in hospital or clinic	—
Bad conditions (Barrens, slums, etc.)	+2
Terrible conditions (cesspool, sewer, etc.)	+4
Character was magically healed of half or more of the damage	–4
Character was magically healed of some of the damage	–2
Character has dermal plating	+3
Character has dermal sheathing or some form of semi-artificial skin	+2
Character has proper healing salve for dermal plating or dermal sheathing	–2

After making the test, count the successes and consult the Scarring Table.

A Terrible scar is large, ugly, and impossible not to notice. A Major scar refers to noticeable disfigurement or discoloration. A Noticeable scar is visible but not particularly noteworthy. A Minor scar is barely noticeable. Minor cosmetic surgery can eliminate all except Terrible scars, if the player character wishes to pay for it. Minor invasive cosmetic surgery can reduce a Terrible scar to a Minor one (see **Elective Surgery**, pp. 114–115, **SRII**).

SCARRING TABLE

Number of Successes	Scar
0	Terrible
1–2	Major
3–4	Noticeable
5+	Minor

CYBERWARE AND BIOWARE

Bioware may have greatly reduced effects on heavily cybered characters. In some instances, bioware and cyberware may produce adverse reactions. The following text applies to biotech described in the **Shadowtech** sourcebook. Bioware items not mentioned in this section function normally, regardless of a character's cybertech implantations.

ADRENAL PUMP

The less meat there is to stimulate, the less effective adrenal augmentation becomes. Assuming that an adrenal pump works at 100 percent efficiency in a body with no cyberware, the gamemaster should reduce the efficiency of the adrenal pump by 15 percent for each cyberlimb, 10 percent for each partial cyberlimb, 5 percent for each cyberhand or foot, and by 20 percent for a cybertorso. Reductions for partial cyberlimbs and cyberhands and feet are cumulative.

The total reduction of efficiency determines how much of the bioware's usual bonus the cybered character receives. A cyberleg, a cyberhand, and a cybertorso reduce the adrenal pump's efficiency by 40 percent (15 + 5 + 20 = 40). If a character has those cyber enhancements, he receives only 60 percent of the usual bonus provided by his adrenal pump. This reduction would affect a Level 2 adrenal pump as follows. The usual bonuses conferred by such a pump are +2 to Quickness, Strength, and Willpower, and +4 to Reaction. Sixty percent of +2 equals 1.2 (2 x .60 = 1.2), rounded down to 1, and so the bonus to Quickness, Strength, and Willpower drops to +1. Sixty percent of +4 equals 2.4 (4 x .60 = 2.4), rounded down to 2; the character's Reaction bonus drops to +2.

The Reaction Enhancer system described on p. 38 of **Comfortably Numb** reduces the normal bonuses for the adrenal pump by 50 percent.

Adrenal pumps do not function in conjunction with move-by-wire systems, because the combination produces violent and uncontrollable responses completely out of proportion to stimuli and the body's natural reflexes. Such catastrophic overstimulation is totally unworkable.

DAMAGE COMPENSATOR

The damage compensator does not affect the functions of cyberlimbs or reduce damage to them.

ENHANCED ARTICULATION

This systemic implant cannot be integrated into a cyberlimb. The Reaction gain conferred by enhanced articulation is lost if the character gains a Reaction bonus from Quickness-enhanced cyberlimbs or if more than two of the character's limbs are partly or wholly replaced by cyberlimbs. Because enhanced articulation is system-wide and different limbs do not have different Reaction Ratings (the mind truly boggles at this possibility), there is no need to come up with formulas for individual limbs.

MUSCLE REPLACEMENT/AUGMENTATION

Standard rules for muscle replacement (p. 249, **SRII**) and muscle augmentation (p. 35, **Shadowtech**) assume that the muscle/strength increase is applied equally across all the muscle

groups in the body. Unless a character already has one or more cyberlimbs, muscle replacement or augmentation can only be accomplished in this way. The presence of cyberlimbs reduces the Essence Cost and the purchase price for each point of muscle replacement or augmentation by 20 percent (round fractions up) per cyberlimb. Note that this rules clarification may create a strength imbalance; different parts of the body may have different strength bonuses. For applicable rules, see **Strength Enhancements**, p. 50.

SUPRATHYROID GLAND

Cyber enhancements affect suprathyroid glands in the same manner as adrenal pumps. Note that only major-scale bodyware/cyberlimb replacements render the suprathyroid gland useless. Like the adrenal pump, suprathyroid glands are incompatible with the move-by-wire systems.

SYNAPTIC ACCELERATOR

Synaptic accelerators may be integrated with move-by-wire systems only with considerable difficulty. To date, medical specialists have successfully combined only Level 1 synaptic accelerators with move-by-wire systems, and the integration of the two requires extreme care. If a character wants the combination, triple the normal cost for the synaptic accelerator. Move-by-wire systems can only be implanted simultaneously with synaptic accelerators. Characters who already possess accelerators cannot receive move-by-wire systems, and vice versa.

SYNTHACARDIUM

The customary bonus synthacardiums provide to Athletics-based tests is not cumulative with any bonuses from cyberlimbs.

CYBERWARE AND SOCIAL INTERACTION

As noted in various **Shadowrun** products, heavily chromed individuals tend to suffer social disapproval (when did you last have a fun conversation with someone who looked like a vending machine?). To simulate this reality, the gamemaster may use the following optional rules in appropriate social situations and when cybered characters are dealing with contacts.

SOCIAL SITUATIONS

In some social situations, having lots of cybertech is no big deal. The Johnson hiring runners may actually be reassured at the sight of would-be employees who look like they can really take care of themselves (he may decide he doesn't like them much as human beings, but that's not the point). Interrogations and other situations where runners are in a position of strength, or dealings with people who are used to heavily chromed individuals (the military, research scientists, and so on) also pose few problems.

However, excessive cyberware should be a liability for most casual social interactions. If a runner is trying to get some information from a stranger or a person he knows only slightly at a

CONTACT REACTIONS TABLE

Successes	Effect
4+	Contact remains unaffected.
3	Contact is slightly aloof or cold.
2	Contact initially attempts to avoid the runner. Apply a +1 modifier to target numbers for all subsequent Charisma or Social Skill tests.
1	Contact consistently attempts to avoid the runner without going to excessive lengths. Apply a +1 modifier to the target number for all subsequent Charisma or Social Skill tests.
0	Contact shuns runner and refuses to help him unless coerced.

shop or in a bar, walking in with a look that says "I use metal polish every day" is a real no-no. Gamemasters may reflect this in game play with the following modifier to Charisma or Charisma-based Skill Tests: +1 to all target numbers for every 2 points of Essence (or portion thereof above .5) below the normal Essence Attribute of 6.

The gamemaster may adapt this modifier based on the visibility of the cyberware. For cyberware that is invisible to normal senses, such as headware memory, skillsofts, cortex bombs, and the like, the +1 modifier may not apply at all. Datajacks should be ignored; these items are so common that they cause no social disapproval (unless the character has them mounted somewhere very strange indeed). Wired reflexes and cyberware that primarily affects movement, such as move-by-wire systems, *should* have a modifier; even though the actual cyberware may not be visible, its effects are immediately apparent. Disguised cyberware, such as cyberlimbs with semi-natural covering, may or may not require a modifier depending on the results of Perception Tests needed to spot them.

The +1 modifier should apply to any cyberware the gamemaster deems flagrant in appearance (lurid cybereyes, steely cyberarms over which a character wears nothing but headache-inducing short-sleeved Hawaiian shirts, and so on).

Additional modifiers are the gamemaster's call, depending on the situation. For example, a runner chatting at the bar with the staff of a newssheet devoted to cutting-edge cybertech is not going to attract anywhere near the negative attention of a street samurai conversing with back-to-nature elves who shudder at the very thought of implanting metal into themselves. However, the gamemaster should always apply a minimum modifier of +1 for a character with Essence loss greater than 3.0, unless the circumstances are exceptional.

Subtle and tricky situations arise when characters use offsetting factors such as tailored pheromones (p. 18, **Shadowtech**). Such things can completely eliminate the Charisma penalty of obvious cyberware. However, the person talking to such a runner should not behave as they would to a normal individual. They *know* the runner is strange and different, not quite human (or metahuman) in the same way they are. The possible situations that can arise are infinite, and the gamemaster must use his own judgment when dealing with them.

CONTACTS

Runners with excessive cyberware appear dangerous to other people and may lose contacts as people begin to shun them. Contacts who work with cybertechnology or cybered individuals on a regular basis may have no problem dealing with heavily cybered runners, but in other cases the gamemaster should consider making over-chromed runners work hard to keep the contacts they have. The gamemaster should require a periodic Charisma Test to see if a given contact is still friendly to the runner, or if the contact will take at least minimal steps to avoid that runner because of a developing aversion. The base target number for these tests is 3. Apply Essence-loss modifiers as described in **Social Situations** as well. For contacts, however, the +1 modifier should apply even in cases where cyberware is not obvious. This rule assumes that a given runner's contact knows the runner well enough or has been around him enough to see, feel or intuit the effects of any cyberware. In general, this Charisma Test should be made once per run, when the runner first seeks out the contact. If a gamemaster has players whose runners go out every weekday and night, the test may be made less frequently. These tests should be made for all characters whose Essence loss from cyberware implantation exceeds 0.5; datajacks can be ignored at the gamemaster's discretion. The effects of the Charisma Test depend on the number of successes achieved, as indicated on the Contact Reactions Table.

A cybered runner should not lose more than one contact per test period. The gamemaster may make fresh tests for all contacts the first time they meet the runner after he has additional cyberware implanted, using the Contact Reactions Table to determine their reactions.

The gamemaster may allow runners to avoid these penalties if they make active attempts to keep on their contacts' good sides. Make the players work at this; simply buying their contacts drinks or handing over money won't do. Runners must use a more personal touch—a thoughtful gift, some news about someone important to that contact, or some other action to demonstrate to the contact that the humanity they sensed was absent from the runner is not actually lost.

PART 2: CYBERMANCY

My first thought was not my own. It was my voice, my words, but the intention to express those ideas and memories was not mine. Or at least, it was not mine as I once understood myself to be.

>>>>>(This is the file I've been waiting for, though it took longer to get than I'd expected. I suppose it was foolish of me to think it would turn up as quick as I'd hoped. How long does it take to recover from cybersurgery on the scale Hatchetman must have undergone? I figured that with the amount of money the Unnamed Corp had probably thrown into this, they'd just add a little magical healing to the budget and get the patient up and around quickly. It didn't occur to me that it might not be that simple.

In the meantime I pulled some strings, called in some favors and markers, and acquired some access time in the Nexus to see what I could dig up about what might be happening to Hatchetman and what implications it might have. That information and my thoughts on it are in the file marked Cybermancy. That file also includes info on a couple of pieces of technology I ran across during my research. I figured knowledge of them might be useful to anyone reading this.

This file was delayed because Hatchetman needed some time to get it together enough to set down this material. And he also had to get around the Corp-With-No-Name to get it out of the clinic. Apparently the corp increased security dramatically after he sent his first message. That may be my fault, because I went ahead and posted the first part of this screed assuming the second part would arrive almost immediately. But I got all of it eventually, so I suppose it doesn't matter. I'm not going to comment on exactly how Hatchetman got this drek out in the first place—the corp's security can do without any leads in searching for the courier. Let's just say someone's alive to the implications of this datasnatch and isn't resting easy at night.

Anyway, here's Hatchetman's message, word for word. All the omissions, starts and stops and digressions are the author's. Also, the original file was recorded in bits and pieces—a nuance that I know will get lost in the reformatting. I've put in a "———" marker where those spaces are. The file was badly and strangely compressed and encrypted, so I'm not even sure

BERGTING

of the original order of the pieces. They appear as I saw them when I first unfolded the file. Hatchetman may have intended the pieces to fall this way, but I can't say for sure.

Like the first "bio-file" Hatchetman wrote, I've locked this one to read-only. Don't hack in. Just read and learn.)<<<<<

—Captain Chaos (02:15:47/03-24-56)

I knew those thoughts and those words, and I knew they had once belonged to me. But they were mine in the same way that the memories of a trid I once saw were mine. Not that I can't tell the difference between trid memories and things I did—I can. It's just that my own memories somehow lack clarity.

Has my past become fuzzy, or has the present become so much more clear?

Twice I've found myself waiting for a heartbeat that never came …

For awhile—I cannot say how long—my only sense was a trideo feed from a camera in the isolation bay. It was pointed away from me, so I couldn't hear anyone unless they stood right in front of the camera. All I could see was the stainless-steel plating of the wall, a white piece of connecting plastic that ran along the wall at waist height, the edges of dark metal and dark plastic ceiling tile and the glare from an inset light. There was a stylish plastic table, and a metal stool next to it. Sometimes a clipboard or a piece of gear lay on the table. Usually it was bare.

That was all I saw for a long time.

The first voice I heard was a woman's—deep, throaty, and amused. I think she said something about muffins.

Things come back to me without warning when I've stopped paying attention to the world around me. So far I've been able to keep it straight that these things have already occurred and are not here and now, but it's hard. Sometimes I hear voices and I have to look around for my mother, my brother Fizz, or Traci, or one of the others. I know they're not there, but I have to look just in case. This only happens when I stop thinking …

My room has no mirrors in it. The walls are brushed metal so I cannot see myself in them. I know I am taller than I was.

Vincent was kind. I never should have done that. But I did. The sad thing is, even the voices in my head cannot help me remember her name.

It was Dara.

They showed me my arm. It's not mine, but it moves when I want it to. That hand flexes when I want it to flex, and I feel pain in it when I slam it against the metal bar. It can't be mine. They say they'll cover it over.

Did I ever tell you how Fizz died?

We were taking care of some business, something unfortunate that a mutual friend had gotten into. It was in Tacoma, down by the docks. No, wait …

The doctor told me that the voices were to remind me of who I was. I asked him why he thought I might forget, and then he said the voices were there to remind me that I was alive.

Of course I'm alive, I said. We're talking, aren't we?

He agreed, but said some people would argue the point. Not that we were talking, but that I was alive. I told him I didn't understand. He said that death is traditionally defined as the cessation of certain kinds of brain activity, and that was where the definitional problem came in.

I think I held up my hand as I told him to stop, because he sounded surprised. I couldn't see my hand. I couldn't even see him—it was one of those days where I could only hear. They told me later it was a cable problem. I told him I didn't care what the definitions were, and I asked him if I was alive.

He said yes.

I asked him if I was going to stay alive.

He said yes, as long as I remembered.

Remembered what, I asked.

Remembered that I was alive, he answered.

I don't feel like me, but I look like me. I'm taller, I think. I feel taller. I move more smoothly than I ever did before, quickly and quietly and without error or misstep. They seem pleased by that. I can feel the extra weight on my body. One of the nurses said I weighed about three times what I used to, and that I'd have to remember that. More things to remember.

I can hear better, see better, and react faster. My mind is sharper, my attention focused, and my perceptions more detailed. They tell me I will be able to fire a combat shotgun at full rate and it will barely buck. And I don't have to breathe if I don't want to, at least for short periods.

Sometimes I forget. Sometimes, when nothing is happening, my mind starts to slip away. Lethargy grows, and I have no desire to stop it. The voices come then, the memories of things that happened years ago or minutes ago. I can't tell which. Little pieces of me tell me to stay and not move on, not to go away. Sometimes I start feeling warm when this happens.

Late one night, someone came and spoke to me. It might have been Priest, but I don't think so. He's gone. It might have been my memories telling me something I'd forgotten, but I'm not sure. Whoever it was came in without my seeing him enter and left without my seeing him leave.

He told me that I wanted to die. My body and spirit knew that I should be dead, and only tricks of magic and technology were keeping me alive. I was caught on the edge of death and held there by my own willpower. The voices, some of the tech in my body, and apparently some magic—though none of the doctors or nurses had ever mentioned magic—existed to help me fight the urge to die.

Ultimately, he said, nothing anyone did could keep me alive if I did not want to live. He said the time might come when I would no longer want life. Then, he said, I would find it easy to slip away.

I look big, and I move well. Too well. There is something about me that makes people shy away. It's not how I look—at least, I don't think so. Surprisingly, I don't look that different—I look like myself, only larger. I have a vague memory of a hand, a hand that frightened me because of how it looked, and someone saying they'd fix it. Cover it. Something like that. I don't remember why it frightened me. Some people have told me that my face isn't as expressive as it once was, but I can live with that. They also told me it cost a lot more to make me look like me, and that I almost ended up looking—different. I don't know what to say to that.

When I walk through the halls, people move aside almost instinctively as I ap-proach. A few speak to me, but even they seem ill at ease.

Walking the halls—that's when I discovered the detail problem.

When I first reawakened, I noticed that I seemed more aware. The world looked more crisp and bright, and I was more conscious of it. As I walked the halls I tried to notice things about people. I saw one nurse, a slight girl who I knew couldn't be as young as she seemed because everyone here knew too much. I watched her. I studied the asymmetrical bend of the wire in her earrings, the scar along the left side of her jaw line that her makeup hid from all but me, the faint shades of dark brown at the roots of her red hair, the slight difference in the sheen of her replacement cybereyes, the chipped nail on the ring finger of her left hand, and the fading bruise on her left wrist. I noticed these things, absorbed them, reviewed them, considered them, and then I noticed the voices. Many sets of them, inside and outside my head.

Suddenly people were there, doctors and nurses pulling and pushing me, attaching devices and running bits of equipment over my body. I could hear my friends from preschool, the derelict with the three-legged dog who used to curse at us kids, and I could remember my own heartbeat.

I had gotten lost and nearly drifted away. I'd become so immersed in every little thing about this woman that I'd forgotten everything else. I'd forgotten to remember to be alive.

I took a deep breath then—my first in nearly half an hour, they told me later. The nurse I'd gotten lost in was halfway across the room behind me, but I could smell the chemicals in her hair. I turned to look at her. She stood a little distance away from some orderlies and other nurses, looking over at me.

She smiled, hesitantly. I tried to smile back. I don't know if I managed.

I was alive.

>>>>>(The file ends there. I've been told Hatchetman is no longer at the clinic. He was released a few weeks ago, but he hasn't gone home or contacted any of his friends. I don't know what this means.

If any of you hear from him, please let us know.)<<<<<

—Captain Chaos (02:22:06/03-24-56)

CYBERMANCY

There comes a time when you have to stop thinking about adding machine to the man and look at adding man to the machine."
—Dr. Robert Martin, University of Berlin, 2055

>>>>>(This file is a compilation and abridgment of the information I gathered while waiting for the second file from Hatchetman. I can vouch for my research, but I can't vouch for the complete accuracy of what I dug up. All of this information is heavily guarded and protected by all the megacorps involved, and I can't say with any certainty how many false trails I picked up without knowing it—hopefully, not too many.

I wish I could say that this file will give you all the ins and outs and nuts and bolts of cybermancy. Unfortunately, it can't—partly because I couldn't get to everything there is (or might be) to know, and partly (I suspect) because the people working with this arcane drek don't know all the implications of the genie they've let out of the bottle. This file should, however, give you enough of a background and basic understanding of what's happened to Hatchetman to make your sleep considerably more troubled. Wherever necessary, I asked people whose expertise I know and trust to clarify or expound on parts of the discussion. This file is flagged as read-write, so feel free to post as normal.)<<<<<

—Captain Chaos (03:17:35/03-24-56)

The word "cybermancy" is so new that you won't even find it in the real-time edition of *WorldWide WordWatch*. Here's the definition I came up with:

Cybermancy *n.* A multidisciplinary science that combines aspects of biology, cybernetics, and the magical healing arts in order to merge man and machine.

That's my take on it, at least. I suspect some of the people actually involved in it might argue with me, but since they're not talking my explanation holds for now.

NO FEAR

>>>>>(Think anyone working on this drek will post here?)<<<<<
—Chuck-Chuck Razool (05:45:30/04-06-56)

>>>>>(Not bloody likely.)<<<<<
—Findler-man (03:54:47/04-07-56)

I can hear some of you raising the question already—how is cybermancy different from cybernetics as we know it? Technically, cybernetics is the design and creation of the parts themselves. Cybermancy deals primarily with getting the chrome in the body and keeping it there.

The conventional wisdom has it that the body can only hold so much cyberware before it simply gives up and dies, even if it was completely healthy right up to the moment of death. Cybermancy is trying to prove the conventional wisdom wrong, or at least get around it. At its heart, cybermancy means keeping the body alive after it should be dead. I'm not talking about artificial life support either, at least not in the conventional sense of respirators and external heart systems.

>>>>>(It's just a question of biological rejection. Where's the problem?)<<<<<
—Unicorn (05:45:48/04-01-56)

>>>>>(Read on, ugly one-horned mule.)<<<<<
—Ridley (03:55:06/04-02-56)

Those of you who cruise these boards regularly might remember a post to the **Tír na nÓg** file back in August of '54 from one Doc Dresden. The post was his response to a mention in that file that the Tír na nÓg elves shy away from cyberware because it "reduces sacred essence," which they equate with spirit. Doc D posted an abridged version of Doctors John Clark and Terri-Anne Clybourne's Essence-Integrity Theory, which appeared in the April '53 *Journal of Metaphysical Proceedings*. Here's that abridgment again:

We all carry a metapsychic blueprint, an astral template, conceived with our physical selves and borne until our deaths. This template represents not only who we are, but what we might have been had our bodies and spirits developed unhampered from birth. This aural template, our essence, also connects us to the mystical world. For most people, essence envelops and sustains them throughout life, but they derive no power from it. For a magician, the aural template serves as the circuitry through which magical power flows. It connects the inner world with the outer in a direct, tangible way.

In the past, metaphysicists have warned of the associative damage done to the aural template through the implantation of cybernetics and bioware. Though such warnings have validity, we believe the reasoning behind them to be inaccurate.

Rather than damaging the aural template, we believe the damage associated with cyber- and bioware and the resultant loss in magical potency results from the deviation between an individual's aural template and his body. In effect, the implantation of artificial enhancements creates a new body, or physical template, that differs from the aural template. The greater the deviation, the less efficient the transfer of mana from the aural to the physical becomes.

The adaptability of the aural template seems to explain why mundane individuals seem to suffer less from bioware than magicians. This adaptability is inversely related to an individual's ability to work magic. If the aural template's fabric is stressed by the workings of magic, it becomes less adaptable and therefore cannot compensate for even relatively minor physical deviations caused by bioware.

It seems Clark and Clybourne were right. I asked my good friend Magister to translate the above academese into words more easily understood by the average Joe and explain the theory's implications.

HOW CYBERMANCY WORKS

by Magister

According to Clark and Clybourne, the problem with cyberware is the changes it makes between the aura and the body. You can get away with altering your body up to a point; but eventually you reach a threshold where the difference between the aural template and the physical body is so great that the spirit slips away or dissolves (depending on whether or not you believe in a hereafter). When the spirit leaves, the body dies.

>>>>>(I don't buy it. It's simple rejection. Happens with replacement organs all the time.)<<<<<
—Unicorn (05:58:02/04-01-56)

>>>>>(If that's true, why doesn't it follow the same pattern? Why is it that after a point, the body dies no matter what you put into it? How come that only happens at a certain point? Cyberware rejection happens all the time, but it's easily tempered by treatment these days. This kind of reaction isn't. Once you hit that threshold, you're dead. Or you were, until now.)<<<<<
—Orson (23:12:01/04-02-56)

Exhaustive research has shown that the threshold is an absolute. It does not vary among the (meta)human races, and with the exception of certain paranormal creatures and beings it does not vary anywhere in Nature. A human and a troll can take the same amount of cyberware before death, despite their obvious differences in size and mass.

>>>>>(I can hear all the racists out there grinding their teeth over that last bit.)<<<<<
—Findler-man (04:01:18/04-07-56)

This conclusion proves to me that the strength of the spirit is universal. If you replace an arm on a troll and an arm on a dwarf, the loss to the spirit is virtually identical. The physical arm apparently has little to do with it—it's the symbolic loss of an arm that matters. In a spiritual sense, an arm is an arm regardless of whose it may be. The loss is the same, and the damage is the same.

This kind of thing gets very metaphysical, and for some may border on the religious. I leave those implications to people who enjoy talking about such things. For the rest of us, the data means that the threshold is definable. We know when death from essence loss occurs. Even taking into account such variables as the skill of the doctor, the conditions of the cybersurgery, and so on, a definable threshold raises the interesting possibility that the threshold can be managed—tampered with, even changed. Based on the information Captain Chaos passed on to me, playing with the threshold is what cybermancy is all about.

>>>>>(Let them die, I say. If that's what's supposed to happen, let it happen.)<<<<<

—Doktor K. (14:48:32/04-05-56)

>>>>>(Hasn't the entire history of medicine involved finding ways to cheat death?)<<<<<

—Leather & Lace (21:28:36/04-05-56)

>>>>>(Actually, the entire history of medicine has involved the medical profession protecting its own privileges and prestige, as shown by the historical fact that at any given time the majority of "medicines" available have had no demonstrated therapeutic value whatsoever.)<<<<<

—MesoStim (19:12:05/04-24-56)

Normally, beyond the threshold point the spirit slips away. Cybermancy uses advanced techno-magical techniques to fool it into staying. How the cybermancers manage to do this could fill up this datastore with terapulses of equations, theory, technobabble and outright guesses. (One prevalent theory the good Captain ran across fools the spirit by using nanotechnology to continually update the subject's DNA sequence. Truthfully, the science of all that is way beyond me.) Whatever the techniques actually being used, cybermancy can keep the aura and the body together, to a point somewhere beyond the usual threshold. Of course at this stage the science of cybermancy has its limits, too—even the topnotch cybermancers can't keep the spirit around indefinitely. At least I don't think so.

>>>>>(Give 'em a coupla years. This science thing is starting to scare me.)<<<<<

—Ghoulie (10:13:54/04-04-56)

>>>>>(Starting to scare you??)<<<<<

—'Shroom (23:54:48/04-05-56)

The development of cybermancy raises an even more interesting question: do we really need an aura to stay alive? Can we combine technology and magic to keep the body going after death? Will we reach a point some day soon when we can all exist just fine without one? Technically, yes we can keep the body going. As to existing just fine without an aura, however, the picture gets considerably more complex—and more than a little frightening.

Once the spirit has departed, the flesh begins to fail. The body can be sustained by combinations of technology and magic, but after a certain point there is no purpose in doing so. Rather than expending the effort necessary to maintain dead flesh indefinitely, it is simpler and, to some extent, more reliable to replace the offending bit of meat with a machine. This applies to all parts of the body with one exception—the brain.

No matter how hard people have tried—and I've seen more information on the subject than you'd care to know about—the brain cannot be sustained mechanically or mystically after death. It quickly degrades, and computers and machines can perform only a handful of its most minor functions. Overall, the computer is no match for the human brain—not now, despite our impressive advances in computer technology, and I suspect not ever.

To sum up, it is possible to maintain the body after death by using some combination of technological and mystical techniques to fool the spirit into remaining. It is a tricky procedure at best, rife with complications depending on how far past the threshold the body has gone. But it can be done. I will leave the debate over whether or not it *should* be done to others.

>>>>>(HOLY DREK! I just realized something! I was on a run not too long ago and the corp provided some "special backup." Let me tell you, these guys were WEIRD. They were big, walking muscle-machines that stared at you all the time like you were talking a different language.

At the tail end of the run, the Johnson gave instructions to one of these muscle-machines. I couldn't hear what he said, but the big guy just stared at the Johnson for a few moments and then walked away. The Johnson didn't know I was looking, but I could tell he was shaken by having to deal with the brute. After the muscle-machine turned away, the Johnson spiked his cigarette into the ground and muttered something about "fraggin' zombie." Could the muscle-men be what this Magister guy's talking about?)<<<<<

—Weasel Boy (21:09:00/04-02-56)

>>>>>(Where you been, Weasel Boy?? I used the word "zombie" way back in the Cutting Edge file. I've heard that term rattled around for a year or so now; it hasn't quite filtered down to the streets, but I suspect it will soon. Cyberzombies, that's what they call them. More machine than man.)<<<<<

—Findler-man (06:18:54/04-03-56)

>>>>>(Ain't that gonna cause some confusion between them and real zombies?)<<<<<

—Dwek (12:38:40/04-03-56)

>>>>>(There ain't no such thing as "real zombies" you—you dwek!)<<<<<

—Fabber (21:03:57/04-05-56)

>>>>>(A few years ago I heard some rumors about brutes called "hellions" that sounded an awful lot like Weasel's zombies. Does anyone else remember this?)<<<<<

—Steel Lynx (16:08:54/04-06-56)

>>>>>(I remember them. Boy, do I. I'll bet they were forerunners of zombies. It seems too long ago for it to be the same thing, but the hellions could have been the first test of cybermancy. I'd heard they were a little unstable.)<<<<<

—Findler-man (23:36:28/04-07-56)

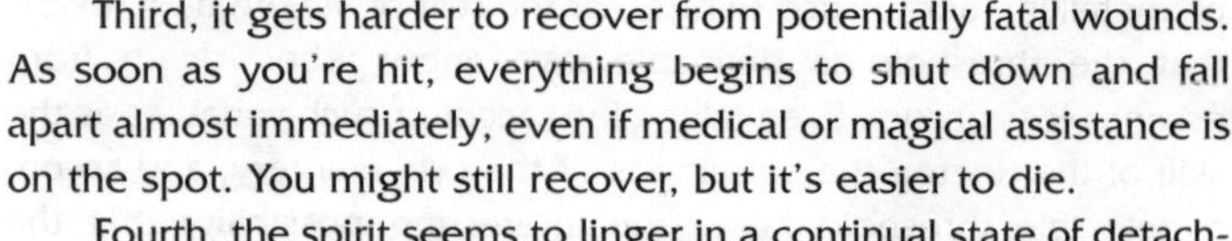

Okay, folks, it's Captain Chaos again. You've read the Essence-Integrity Theory and Magister's thoughts on the subject. Want to know what it all means for people like us? Quite a bit—some good (maybe) and an awful lot that isn't very pretty.

The first and most obvious plus—for some people, anyway—is that cybermancy lets you use more cyberware. The material I dug up tossed around quite a range of vague numbers, but it seems to boil down to somewhere between 15 and 30 percent more than is possible under normal circumstances.

>>>>>(Fraggin' TERRIFIC!)<<<<<
—Sharp Ax (20:00:23/04-06-56)

Another possible plus is a side effect of the techniques used, or maybe just the natural consequence of having so much tech in the body. Apparently, cybermancy makes the subject inherently more resistant to magic. As I understand it, using magic involves aura-synchronization to properly target a spell or casting. Cybermancy somehow throws that out of balance, so magic has a lot less of an effect on a cybermantically sustained individual.

>>>>>(Oh, yeah!)<<<<<
—Bad-Ass Backlander (05:50:01/04-05-56)

There may be other advantages to undergoing cybermancy, but I didn't find them. Considering the enormity of the disadvantages, I doubt *any* so-called advantages are really worth it.

>>>>>(Uh-oh.)<<<<<
—Bad-Ass Backlander (05:51:03/04-05-56)

>>>>>(Frag it, sign me up!)<<<<<
—Sharp Ax (20:02:02/04-06-56)

In fact, cybermancy presents so many disadvantages that I wonder how anyone in their right mind can even consider going this route.

>>>>>(As if some people have a choice.)<<<<<
—Hangfire (21:17:55/04-02-56)

First, there's the simple fact that the body should be dead. To keep it alive, reservoirs are built into it to provide dosages of various medicines needed to keep the body functioning. But that medicine has to be refilled constantly, which means getting and spending lots of nuyen.

Second, cybermancy apparently poses a long-term threat of cancer, though no one seems to know for sure how long-term it is. Cybermantic techniques appear to involve mucking around with the subject's DNA somehow, and over time that raises the risk of cancerous mutation.

Third, it gets harder to recover from potentially fatal wounds. As soon as you're hit, everything begins to shut down and fall apart almost immediately, even if medical or magical assistance is on the spot. You might still recover, but it's easier to die.

Fourth, the spirit seems to linger in a continual state of detachment, leading to the mental malaise that Hatchetman talked about. Without stimulation, the mind wanders, and the spirit wanders as well unless it's caught in time. The body is continually monitored, and so support systems automatically kick in when the mind decides to go for a jander. Remember those voices Hatchetman talked about? They came from a piece of cyberware called an Invoked Memory Stimulator (IMS) that randomly activates the subject's memories. According to the literature I've read, the IMS is usually enough to bring the zombie back from the brink—but not always. Mental overstimulation is also a problem—the mind can get lost in minutiae without realizing it. When this happens, the spirit wanders and once again the IMS kicks in to stop it.

>>>>>(Interesting. This implies that keeping the spirit around is a matter of willpower. The IMS seems to sort of kick-start the will.)<<<<<
—Vooch (21:02:47/04-04-56)

Fifth, the subject's will to live drops like the proverbial rock.

>>>>>(Uh-oh ...)<<<<<
—Vooch (21:03:19/04-04-56)

The subject doesn't consciously want to die, but his ability to exert any mental strength goes way, way down. The IMS and some magical techniques apparently counteract this to some extent, but all the material I've read cited this lack of will to live as a major, ongoing concern. That tells me they haven't beat the bugs yet, at least not in this area.

Sixth, don't expect people to like you any more. They'll shun you. You'll give people the creeps. People who've known you all your life will suddenly be unable to stomach your presence. Think about it—would *you* feel comfy pounding a few beers in the company of a schizoid psychopath with zero empathy capacity and the ability to demolish the bar inside of five seconds?

>>>>>(Heck, we do that all the time down here in Texas. It's called socializing.)<<<<<
—Potatoe Head (20:15:11/05-03-56)

Finally—and this one might just end the whole matter for any of you seriously thinking about going this route (provided you could find a corp willing to do it for you)—the magical techniques used on the subject have one last interesting side effect. The subject becomes permanently astrally active. I know this seems to contradict my earlier statement about increased resistance to magic, but the two are not mutually exclusive. The magic used on the subject gives him a permanent astral presence of sorts, even as it makes him more resistant to other people's magic. Definitely a two-edged sword.

>>>>>(The wiser among you will realize that the risks of cybermancy are currently so great that the old dictum about surgery being the last refuge of the gambling man is dead right. You can do it, but it's going to get you. "It" may be chronic dissociation syndrome, the death of the will, incurable cancer, death at the hands of the astral predators attracted to you, death from unhealable wounds. And you won't go gently into that good night, not at all. Cheat death, and the dying will be more horrific than your worst nightmares.

But it may not always be so. The mages who know cybermantic rituals are always striving to improve them. Over time, it may become increasingly possible to sustain existence as a cyberzombie—the term used in those trash-hip tridsheets by people who know nothing.

So don't do it now. If you're going to do it, wait a while. And God help you.)<<<<<

—Umkanwe (01:00:32/03-16-56)

>>>>>(God is dead.)<<<<<

—Nihilist (04:17:17/03-22-56)

>>>>>(Nah, he's just got sub-zero Essence >chuckle<)<<<<<

—Papal Bulldrekker (15:19:10/04-01/56)

WHERE TO FIND IT

Even with all the disadvantages of cybermancy, I suspect far too many folks out there may be far too willing to give up their humanity for a little more edge. Lucky for them that's not going to happen—at least, not for awhile. According to my research, only five or six clinics in the world perform this kind of operation. These are the no-longer-mythical delta clinics, and all but one (or maybe two) belong to major megacorps. As for where to find them, all I have is rumors of general locations (and I mean general!).

Fuchi has two clinics, which shouldn't surprise anyone who's been paying attention to business-as-usual in that corp. The first is controlled by the Villiers faction and exists somewhere in NAN territory. I've heard it's in Pueblo land near Durango, but equally reliable sources put it in the mountains somewhere in Ute territory. Your guess is as good as mine. The second Fuchi clinic is controlled by the Nakatomi family and is reputedly somewhere in the Nagano province of Japan.

Aztechnology reputedly runs a delta clinic, but I couldn't pin down the location. Unsubstantiated rumor has it in Tenochtitlán—who knows?

Saeder-Krupp allegedly runs one in the suburb of Ekrath, near Dusseldorf. Apparently one of the ultra-rich enclaves in that area is simply a cover for the clinic. The fact that SK has one at all is due almost exclusively to their acquisition of the Chinese cyberneticist Wei Xiong Chen a few years back.

The fifth clinic is under the control of the Tír na nÓg government. It supposedly exists somewhere in the province of Donegal, but I found little information beyond circumstantial evidence pointing to such a place. I suspect that, as with Saeder-Krupp, the Tír's control of a delta clinic rests on the expertise of one or two individuals. I picked up vague rumors of a sixth clinic, but no clue as to who might own it or where it might be. For all I know, there isn't one.

>>>>>(I can't believe Transys Neuronet doesn't have one. Get real, chummers.)<<<<<

—Vandal (05:45:32/04-04-56)

>>>>>(I'm sure Transys has some sort of facility, but Cap Chaos only looked for clinics that do delta-grade work on a regular basis. Transys probably does that kind of work occasionally, but not regularly. Who knows—they might be the owners of that quasi-mythical sixth clinic. Or maybe their occasional activities are the source of that rumor.)<<<<<

—Findler-man (21:47:38/04-06-56)

>>>>>(Don't underestimate the boys in Silicon Glen. They designed the first reliable move-by-wire system. Word is now that they're working on what you might call cybermantic power systems: core metabolic cybersystems, both somatic and neural. The old word "cyborg" comes to mind, neh? Because they're out on the edge of the world—heck, Iceland is their nearest neighbor—people tend to forget about 'em, which is pretty much how they like it. I'll do my best to keep you posted about what they get up to.)<<<<<

—MesoStim (16:06:31/04-28-56)

>>>>>(Cybermantic power systems? >drool< Yes! Give me one now! No more of that eat-and-dump routine, just a nice internal nuke powering me around. Time to get those entrails removed.)<<<<<

—PowerMakk (02:27:13/04-29-56)

RAMIFICATIONS

The larger meaning of cybermancy is a question each of us has to answer for ourselves. I suspect the long-term impact of these developments will be significant. We've reached the stage where we can start with a (meta)human being, add machine bit by bit or all at once, and end up with something that isn't (meta)human anymore. In fact, I understand that a few cutting-edge researchers have invented experimental expert systems designed specifically to puppet around a zombie who is truly dead. How long will it be before we get meat/machine bodies being driven around by riggers sitting miles away? How long before man truly becomes obsolete, or his parts become no more than a stepping-stone to the ultimate synthesis of (meta)human and machine?

Maybe I'm being paranoid. Maybe I'll stop worrying when and if I eventually talk to Hatchetman again.

Then again, maybe not.

>>>>>(This transcript of a couple of interesting phone conversations came my way just as I was preparing to post the other material. I won't say how I came by it, but the source is damn reliable. It was encrypted in the original, of course. Static interrupts it in one important spot, and I don't know the names of the people talking (though I have my suspicions, and they're two human mages). No images—these people wouldn't use vidphone links. And once again, read-only format—this seems too important to frag with.)<<<<<

—Captain Chaos (16:28:14/12-11-56)

∞

The real issue is who's doing this. Let's face it, most of the specialists we know are horrified by the use of magic to trap the spirit in a dead body.

Ω

And some of them are taking active steps to deal with that.

∞

Yes, we'll get back to that. But what have you got on this?

Ω

I thought we agreed to trade information at your request. It's up to you to put something up front.

∞

Okay. I know of two organizations that instruct initiates in cybermantic magic—one in Britain, one in South America.

Ω
You have the advantage over me on the former score, though I've heard stories. I know of a third in Azania.

∞
News to me.

Ω
I thought that was the idea.

∞
(Laughs) Let's deal with the one we both know something about. The Azzies.

Ω
Yes. Rumors have been circulating for some while that the Prez popped his clogs some time back and is sustained in some form of death-cheating afterlife. There are a thousand versions, from his disembodied brain lying in a bucket linked to a thousand and one cyberdevices, to his being a spirit-infested zombie shambling around the top level of one of those pyramids.

∞
The zombie thing is a sidetrack.

Ω
Of course. Animating a corpse as the houngans do is an entirely different matter. It's got nothing to do with keeping a spirit tied to a body it should have left. The corpse cadavre has no spirit—it's just a lump of animated meat.

∞
What about the blood magic angle?

Ω
That's a question of how. Enough to say that the human sacrifice tales aren't purely speculative. But we can get down to the how another time. For now, let's keep it to who. Tell me about the Brits.

∞
The Ordo Maximus.

Ω
Surely not?

∞
I have a good contact, an ex-member who went through the preliminary and mid-grade initiations and knows most of the big noises. It's one of the reasons he got out.

Ω
They have a reputation for being a bunch of well-juiced old farts.

∞
That's a useful reputation to have if you mess with cybermantic magic. Keeps other people's attention off you. A lot of the wannabees are juiced old farts, as you put it, or younger versions of them. The OM makes a point of recruiting the sons of rich nobility, letting them into the lowest ranks, and pocketing huge wads of cash for their lifetime membership subscriptions.

Ω
Thus perpetuating the image.

∞
Bingo.

Ω
Comparison with the Azzies makes me wonder about the human sacrifice angle—whether this might be a necessary element, at least in these two instances.

∞
That's complicated. If there's a link with the Brit druids, it would be with the hermetics and definitely not the shamanic Celtic types. Human sacrifice isn't unknown to them, but it's a completely different matter. The hermetics are said to practice human sacrifice, but try saying that in Britain. Your libel laws are something fearsome to behold.

Ω
Is there an association with a corporate interest? Obviously with the Azzies, the cult is the country is the company, if you know what I mean. Are we dealing with the

ÔÊ◊ıÁËÁÓÌ·°‡°ﬂ‡ﬂﬂﬁÓØ∏”∏Ø (Static)

∞
Then that's not clear. How does the Azanian angle shed light on this? Or does it?

Ω
That's wholly different. An Azanian hermetic organization exists whose members know the formulae and rituals for cybermantic magic, but they do not practice it. It's anathema to them. That's not to say there aren't one or two who may have learned what there is to learn and then skipped the roost.

∞
This is pretty much a closed book to me. I know little about these people.

Ω
Characteristic American parochialism. Actually, the Heavenherds are not unhappy about that. So far as I can tell, this organization doesn't proselytize.

∞
Frag, that's a lot of long words for ten seconds on a telephone line. (laughs)

Ω
They don't recruit. They don't have wannabees. They don't take in company mages. Membership is not only exclusive, but hereditary.

∞
So if you want in, forget it unless you have the right genes.

Ω
Correct. Elven genes, of course.

∞
Ah. Now that's different.

Ω
Very different to the Azzies or the Brits.

∞
What do the Cabal think of that?
(Long pause)

Ω
I really wouldn't use that word if I were you.

∞
The encryption on this line—

Ω
I said, *I really wouldn't use that word if I were you.*

∞
Okay. But I can't believe they can overhear on this line.

Ω
I didn't hear that. Now, let's try to sum this up. We reckon there are three hermetic organizations that know cybermantic magic in enough depth to produce mages who can cheat death: the Ordo Maximus, the Azzies, and the Azanian Heavenherds.

∞
Okay.

Ω
The next question is how these guys spread out, and who's working where. How the damn cancer is metastasizing, if you like.

∞
I thought we agreed to deal with the mechanics of it.

Ω
You want to do that first? Okay. Let's get down to that. Ritual magic is the backbone of it, obviously.

∞
I understand we're talking a long, long time here.

Ω
Days, I believe.

∞
And we're certainly talking astral travelling by the magicians involved.

Ω
Not all of them. The circle needs only one to do that. It comes at a late stage of the ritual.

∞
What steps have we identified? I'll start the ball rolling. It's essential, as I understand it, not only to have the meat body of the—what are we going to call him—victim? Idiot?

Ω
Client?

∞
(Laughs) Yeah, right. I didn't know you had a background in the world's oldest profession.

Ω
I beg your pardon?

∞
Marketing (laughs). I mean, "client"!? Marketingspeak. Either that or what your two-bit therapist calls you when he's uncovering all those sad, sleazy little complexes in your head.

Ω
(Chuckles) All right. Let's settle for "subject." Anyway, you've got a lot more shrinks over there than we have over here.

∞
You need more than just the subject for the ritual, so I hear. You also need items that are tied to the individual, that have strong emotional significance. The wedding ring from that terrible first marriage that ended with the subject's wife facedown in the Potomac, or whatever. That kind of thing.

Ω
Not absolutely correct, but it helps.

∞
Why? I don't understand the mechanics of this. Usually you need this kind of thing when you don't have the subject, to provide a ritual link.

Ω
Let's get something straight. Some of the things useful in some rituals—neutral items, like a photograph of the person—are useless for the cybermantic ritual. Only powerfully associated items will do for this one—like the wedding ring example you give. I've even heard of a childhood toy being used.

∞
You're kidding.

Ω
No. A piece of filthy blue blanket. Apparently the guy had kept it as a comfort object all his life, mopped his brow with it when he got stressed. He had strong emotional associations to it.

∞
I've read some material on this. What's this kind of thing called?

Ω
Transitional object. Read up on your object-relations theory.

∞
Transition to what?

Ω
That's not important right now. We're digressing. Anyway, this kind of object improves the chances for success, though it's not critical. As I understand it, by collecting as many of the fragments of a person's emotional life in one place as possible, a greater intensity is achieved which makes the effects of the ritual more powerful.
(Pause)

∞
I'm thinking about that. I don't think I like what just occurred to me.

Ω
Which is?

∞
Sacrifice.

Ω
Correct. The chances are improved by killing someone emotionally significant to the client during the ritual. As I've heard it explained, the emotional linkages of the spirit to the outside world are thus diminished and this makes it easier to focus the remaining spiritual energies within the machine-body. But that would have to be done without the subject's knowledge to avoid major emotional stress, even though the sacrifice takes place in proximity to them.

∞
Why in proximity? I always understood that physical distance didn't matter with such linkages.

Ω
Technically it doesn't. The effect is more on the magicians involved than on the

subject. Having everything within the direct field of attention makes the ritual easier for the participants.

∞
Okay. Well, that's that, then. The next issue is spirits.

Ω
This is getting interesting.

∞
I've heard contradictory rumors about this. Some people say an intercession by some spirit form is necessary, and it has to be a spirit of man. Others say that coercion is possible, that the magician sent into the astral can force a spirit to give up some karma or energy to power the binding of the subject's spirit to the dead body.

Ω
Both are technically possible. The latter is certainly true in some instances. The Azzies, I think, approach things differently.

∞
The blood spirits.

Ω
Yes.

∞
What's the cost to the magician?

Ω
The drain is staggering. That's another reason why the Azzies use human sacrifice, of course.

∞
How else could it be handled?

Ω
The Azanians have an entirely different set of formulae.

∞
True, but you said they don't actually do it. Nice to have some formulae, but without field testing I wouldn't want to risk my soul on it.

Ω
You wouldn't want to do that anyway. But I gather they've been tested.

∞
But you said they don't do this.

Ω
The data are somewhat antiquated.

∞
How antiquated?

Ω
Say ten thousand years or so. So I'm given to understand, at any rate.

∞
Ten thousand years!? That's pre-Babylonian, pre-Sumerian, pre-everything. We're talking Ice Age—guys in bear loincloths carrying stone axes. Are you sure about this?

Ω
I wasn't told the details. Let's just say the source has enough power to make me think he knows what he's talking about.

∞
Did they give you any idea of the principles behind their techniques? I mean, this is vital. We know the Azzies use sacrifice and blood spirits to cope with the drain. I've heard related stories about the Ordo Maximus, though not about blood spirits. If there's a way to handle this without recourse to such horrors, then this puts an entirely different complexion on things.

Ω
I'm not sure about that, but as I understand it a Great Spirit can intercede.

∞
A Great Spirit of Man? Frag, I wouldn't want to try to coerce one of those things.

Ω
Coercion isn't involved.

∞
How could you possibly get one to do this voluntarily?

Ω
It's not a Great Spirit of Man—at least, not as we know it. I'm not really up to the task of describing this properly, I'm afraid. It's one of those ineffability things. (laughs)

∞
Oh, *that's* helpful.

Ω
I think we should talk again when I've looked up some friends regarding cybermancy's spread and development. Not to mention the implications, and what happens to the retained spirit. The karma costs are great, of course, but I want to find out more before we speak again.

∞
Okay. I can do the same. Later.

Second Conversation

∞
Good to hear from you. How's tricks?

Ω
Could be better. Had some trouble with an ally.

∞
Those things can make difficult pets.

Ω
I wouldn't let him hear you call him that. *I* certainly don't think of him that way.

∞
OK, down to business. I've found it difficult to trace the places where cybermantic magic is being taught, or whether there's some kind of hermetic diaspora out there spreading the poison around. Lips are sealed tight on this one. But I did hear certain things about Tir Tairngire.

Ω
That rumor's relatively fresh. It's a little early to be clear about it one way or the other.

∞
The way I hear it, the Princes have an interest in this because of the Azzies, whom they hate with a passion. They could be researching countermeasures or simply trying to understand what's involved.

Ω
The latter is hardly difficult. After all, the various factors involved in the rituals are well known.

∞
True. Let's talk about that some more. It seems that cybermancers are going to an awful lot of trouble for a meager reward. The rituals are difficult, time-consuming, and they involve deathly drains. What's more, they need to be repeated, don't they?

Ω
If the retained spirit develops hazing or terminal dissociation syndrome, there are ways of re-binding it.

∞
And that happens frequently?

Ω
That depends on exactly how much metal is put into the flesh. If the strain of bearing all the metal is very high, then yes, such complications can arise fairly often.

∞
So why bother? It costs the earth in time, money, and resources. It's a short-term fix. What kind of deal is that?

Ω
A lot of people will pay anything to cheat death, if only for weeks or months.

∞
But that's not the point. In some cases, we're talking about people who are quite capable of staying alive. They just want to burden their bodies with ridiculous amounts of cyberware beyond their capacity to tolerate. That's quite different.

Ω
That's rarely the reason for major cybermantic magic, outside of corporate interests. And it isn't the real purpose. Frankly, that kind of thing is just using the meat bodies as experimental objects.

∞
Okay, let's agree to disagree on this. But what's in it for the mages? That's the issue. They have to perform rituals with no benefit to themselves and every chance of things going horribly wrong. Sounds very, very dumb to me.

Ω
I think we've gotten to the crunch. As I understand it, it's partly a power trip. Play with cybermancy and you play with the basic processes of life itself, and the integrity of the spirit. There's no bigger game to play. Especially when you consider the auxiliary aspects—the astral operations, dealing with Great Spirits. The cybermages become intoxicated with power. I think it's that simple. What's that line—"Now I am become death, the destroyer of worlds"?

∞
Familiar to us seps.

Ω
Hindu mythology, actually. Change it to "Now I am become life, the cheater of death" and you've got the cybermancer's power trip.

∞
That doesn't sound right somehow. There has to be more.

Ω
There is.
(Long pause)

∞
Okay. With the Ordo Maximus, I think the power trip may be all there is to it—or pretty much. I think they're just into the power and secrecy number. With the Azzies, we're dealing with something else.

Ω
Right. Though I've uncovered something—we'll come back to it. Go on.

∞
There's—I don't know how to put this—there's almost a religious fervor about it. I mean sure, they have a shamanic priesthood and the state religion and all that drek but I mean *real* fervor. Like the Inquisition or something.

Ω
An interesting parallel, given the role of the Jesuits down there.

∞
Let's not get into that. We'll be here all day. Those South American Jesuits are a little different from the European variety, but you'd know more about that than me.

Ω
Back to the Azzies. You're right. They don't just do it for the sake of power-tripping. The astral conduit is a major factor for them.

∞
I've never gotten close to that.

Ω
Wise man. The astral plane is polluted where they work. They are building some kind of bridge to something, and I think the answer lies there. It's something sinister and dreadful.

∞
We can't discuss that, even on an encrypted line.

Ω
No.

∞
Okay. What about your chummers, the Azanians?

Ω
Different again. We're talking pure knowledge. But a Great One has sometimes—rarely—been sustained in life by binding spirit to body after his death. It's done for symbolic purposes, when the Great One is needed to make a final judgment about some major issue. Choosing a new Governor, that's happened once.

∞
Governor?

Ω
The term used for the head of the Hermetic College. It's more than a purely symbolic role, I have to say. But I'm digressing. It has been done, but my source says their techniques are a body of knowledge that has come to them from ancient history rather than something they chose to develop or work with.

∞
It doesn't sound like these guys are responsible for any spreading of techniques or teaching.

Ω
I doubt it. And that poses a major question for us.

∞
There was something you said you were going to come back to?

Ω
Ah yes, the Ordo. There's a closer affinity between them and the Azzies than you know.

∞
Try me.

Ω
On the blood count.

∞
What do you mean?

Ω
Some people in the Ordo aren't people.

∞
Look, stop talking in riddles and give this to me straight.

Ω
Tut tut, you Americans are so impatient. That's what comes of living in an instant-gratification culture.

∞
Dump the drek.

Ω
(Laughs) All right. There are vampires in the Ordo Maximus. I think they have access to some magical rituals which allow them to use the Essence drain from victims to offset the drain of cybermantic magic. Needless to say, I haven't gotten far trying to find out much more. It's not something I'd want to risk, frankly.

∞
You think that geek de Vries was right, then?

Ω
He got initiated into the middling grades. I think he knew. He may even have met one or two of them. There are a hundred and one tales about how he got infected. If he does know anything about the rituals, he certainly hasn't been spilling the beans.

∞
This is an extra angle I don't want to think too much about.
(Long pause)

∞
Okay, who's putting up some of the big nuyen for all this drek when it gets out into the big wide world? Let's talk about that. I think most people know that Saeder-Krupp's German outfit has money behind the Ordo Maximus.

Ω
No secret there.

∞
I believe the same source is responsible for supplying Villiers and Fuchi with trained personnel. In the latter case, Fuchi mages were trained in the rituals.

Ω
I didn't know that.

∞
I have a damn good source on that. How come you didn't know? You're the one across the Pond (laughs).

Ω
(Laughs) Yeah, but you're the ones who dye the rivers green on St. Paddy's day and I bet you don't know about the Tír na nÓg interest. Not that that's so big a deal, in my opinion—but don't quote me.

∞
Touché. Okay, let's trade. There's an interesting angle on the Fuchi story. A condition of the training is that the mages give up enough of themselves to let the Ordo keep tabs on them, shall we say.

Ω
Aha. Body. Leave us a little something behind when you say goodbye, right?

∞
Right. Ritual magic! "We train your mages, but we make damn sure we can keep an eye on what they're doing, and if we don't like it then we can frag them senseless."

Ω
It's called franchising (laughs).

∞
Sort of, I guess. But why?

Ω
Money. With the SK deal, many millions must have changed hands. Those grimoires cost money. Have you seen the price of orichalcum these days?

∞
Tell me about it. But I suspect the power trip is something to do with it, too. "Now we've got a big corporate buddy and he pays us lots of money, aren't we important?" Even in our world this counts for something.

Ω
That too.

∞
Frankly, I wouldn't want to give up some of my soul to a bunch of fraggin' vampires.

Ω
Presumably the Fuchi mages don't know there are vampires in the Ordo. Most remiss of them (laughs).

∞
The question is, where does this end?

Ω
Until the corps develop true AI, who knows? Once they get that—if they get that—there's no need for the cyberzombies they've been playing with. They might still try to keep VIPs alive beyond the time of natural death, but that's different. Doesn't excite their research scientists so much.

∞
Fine. So we're left with the issue of what this is building up for us all.

Ω
That's why we're talking, really.

∞
The karma hazing is terrifying if it develops as we both fear it will.

Ω
A basic law of the universe is being violated. You can't do that without paying a price. There's some price for the magicians. They can cheat the drain, but they still can't cheat the karma losses.

∞
But they're working on that.

Ω
They're working on forcing it one place farther down the line. The Azzies are developing their sacrifice rituals in this area.

∞
Oh, geez.

Ω
I told you about these people.

∞
Then it's going to get displaced out and beyond. It's going to—frag, where *is* it going to show up?

Ω
The astral. That's what I fear.

∞
Like the hole in the ozone layer?

Ω
Not an exact analogy but it'll do as an image.

∞
What are the exact effects going to be?

Ω
I don't know. Frankly, it's beyond computation. One day we're going to look up and find that we're fragged. People aren't going to return from astral questing and traveling. Like your Amelia Earhart.

∞
Just disappear into the wide blue yonder. Happens already.

Ω
But they'll disappear without a trace—though pollution zones may develop where the hazing shifts around. I don't want to think about this.
(Pause)

Ω
Look, I don't want to mention the Cabal, but I think you heard something about the death of an earlier world.

∞
You're talking about an explosive end to something, some place, where the Cabal lived.

Ω
All right, we know what we're referring to. It wasn't a world, it was only an island on a world. Now think of a world as an island in space. Think of the same thing happening to it.

∞
Come on. Surely that's over the top.

Ω
Where do you want to start? Catastrophic events start with small rumblings and changes.

∞
But we've got to make this known! How can these people do this drek if they know they're bringing *that* down on themselves?

Ω
Oh, they know. The Ordo don't care. They're so arrogant they think it's a million years away and they're doing so little it will never happen. You know—"I can drek in my back yard all I want but pollution is someone else's problem."

∞
That feels right. I mean, that's their trait—arrogance.

Ω
The Azanians know the hazards. That's why they don't do it. That's why they may take steps to stop the people who do.

∞
And that leaves—

Ω
Right. That leaves the rest. That's where the brown stuff's going to hit the fan.

∞
We have some other people to talk to, I think.

Ω
I trust your discretion. We'll speak again.

>>>>>(That's it. If there were any more conversations, I don't have transcripts of them. I don't know who else these two may have spoken with. If anyone out there catches some ripples, any information would certainly be appreciated.

And for all those folks who are going to lose some sleep about the Cabal, I don't know who the frag they mean by that either.)<<<<<

—Captain Chaos (16:44:22/11-11-56)

CYBERMANCY RULES

Until now, the Essence costs of cyberware have limited the amount of cyberware **Shadowrun** characters could possess. Too much cyberware would have reduced the character's Essence below 0, effectively killing the character. The new cybermancy rules, however, enable characters and NPCs to remain "alive" even when their Essence Ratings drop below 0. This means that characters may have a nearly unlimited amount of cyberware—provided they are willing to suffer the various side effects of a cybermantically sustained existence. This section provides rules for performing cybersurgery/cybermancy operations and for these side effects.

FINDING THE RIGHT PLACE

Cybermancy is not available everywhere. In fact, cybersurgery that lowers a character's Essence below 0 can be performed only at delta clinics. Unlike alpha and beta clinics (see pp. 98–99, **Street Samurai Catalog**) characters cannot simply find one of the world's few ultra-secret delta clinics in the local phone book or hear about one from friends. And even if a character does stumble across such a clinic by some rare cosmic coincidence, he cannot simply walk right in and get some work done. Every delta clinic operates under the tight control of a megacorp or nation-state. And the staffs at these clinics do no work for anyone unless their bosses order them to do so.

Therefore, individual gamemasters may decide whether or not to allow cybermancy in their games. Gamemasters who choose to incorporate cybermancy should keep in mind that characters cannot start the game with an Essence Rating below 0. Because of this rule—and because of the potential impact of cybermancy on **Shadowrun** games—cybermancy should be connected to some plot element in a story. Gamemasters should ensure that becoming a cyberzombie is an extended, difficult endeavor full of extensive roleplaying—rather than a matter of simple dice rolls.

For example, a megacorp might provide a player character access to a delta clinic in exchange for some extremely important work, or as a reward for some service yet to be performed. In the

BERGTING

latter case, the character should perform one heck of a service and the megacorp should have an excellent reason for trusting that the runner will come through with the goods. Hatchetman, for instance, performed a run that virtually saved a megacorp from destruction. He got scragged in the process, so his employer decided to reward him by fixing him up better than new. Of course, he was also a convenient guinea pig. Regardless of why the megacorp patched him up in the first place, Hatchetman now owes the corp big time. And the corp expects him to be extremely grateful when they decide to call in that marker.

GROUND RULES

For game purposes, any character who undergoes cybersurgery that reduces his Essence below 0 automatically undergoes cybermancy at the time of the surgery. Only delta clinics may perform these procedures. (No rules are provided for the actual cybermantic ritual. See **Cybermantic Magic**, p. 84, for further information.)

The **Less Than Zero** section provides rules for the cybersurgery/cybermancy procedure. During the procedure, the character receives an implanted automatic-medication system that feeds him special drugs, nutrients, and other substances that will keep his technically dead body alive. The installation of the automatic-medication system costs nothing, but refills of the medicine cost 15,000¥ each and must be purchased every 10 days. If the system runs out of medicine, the character dies immediately. If the corp authorizing the cybersurgery/cybermancy really likes the character, it might swing him a discount of 1D6 x 5 percent on refills. If the corp has something special in mind for the character, it might even pick up the entire tab—a practice that provides the character with a strong motivation for following orders.

LESS THAN ZERO

The cybersurgery/cybermancy procedure is a highly dangerous operation. Unlike regular cybersurgery, which entails no real risk of failure, a character undergoing a cybersurgery/cybermancy operation may well die on the table. The chance of death increases the further the character's Essence drops below 0.

To determine whether or not the character survives the cybersurgery/cybermancy procedure, the gamemaster makes a Biotech or appropriate medical skill test for the performing doctor. The target number for the test is determined by the Essence Rating the character will have if the cybersurgery succeeds. All characters undergoing cybermantic operations automatically receive an invoked memory stimulator (IMS), which carries an Essence Cost of .25 and a price of 137,750¥. Include this Essence Cost when calculating the intended Essence Rating of the operation. Then consult the Cybersurgery/Cybermancy Survival Table for the target number.

To determine target numbers for intended Essence Ratings lower than those listed, continue the progression shown on the table. Technically there is no lower limit, but the possibility of surviving the procedure becomes vanishingly small as the character's Essence drops farther and farther below 0.

Apply all appropriate modifiers listed on the Doctoring Table (p. 113, **SRII**), except for the –2 modifier for intensive care (delta clinics are automatically considered intensive-care facilities). Note that the Willpower-enhancing magic of the cybermantic ritual (**Changes to Willpower**, p. 82) does not apply in this test.

CYBERSURGERY/CYBERMANCY SURVIVAL TABLE

Intended Essence Rating	Target Number
–.05 to –.50	4
–.55 to –1.0	6
–1.05 to –1.50	8
–1.55 to –2.0	10
–2.05 to –2.50	12
–2.55 to –3.0	14

If the test fails, the character dies. That's it. The player cannot spend Karma on the doctor's skill test to enhance his chances. If the test succeeds, the character lives. To determine how well the doctor did his job and modify the actual Essence cost of the procedure accordingly, see **Cybersurgery**, p. 53.

SIDE EFFECTS

The actual cybersurgery/cybermancy operation is by far the riskiest part of using cybermancy. However, a successful operation does not mean the character is in the clear. When a character undergoes a cybermantic operation, he becomes the central participant in a magical ritual intended to fool his spirit into staying with his body. As a result, cybermantic techniques inflict several potentially lethal conditions and side effects on the character. One such condition, the need for an automatic-medication system, is described in **Ground Rules**. Other side effects are described in the following passages.

BETTER OFF DEAD

Ironically, cybermancy makes dying easier for a character, because it reduces the character's Physical Damage Overflow value (Body Rating + 10) by half (round up). (For more information on Physical Damage Overflow, see **Exceeding the Condition Monitor**, p. 111, **SRII**.) The odds are that the character has boosted his Body Rating by at least one piece of cyberware or bioware, so initially this side effect does not pose too much of a problem.

However, every time the character experiences Physical Damage Overflow and is healed or stabilized, the character must make a Willpower Test against a target number equal to twice the amount of overflow damage. If the test fails the character dies, regardless of any magical or mundane healing measures applied. The character may spend Karma to prevent this, and cybermantic adjustments to Willpower apply to the test as well (see **Changes to Willpower**, p. 82).

MAGICAL SIDE EFFECTS

Characters who undergo cybermantic treatment become more resistant to magic. To reflect this side effect, add twice the absolute value of the character's Essence Rating to the target number of any magical test made against him. (The absolute value of –2 is 2, for example.) Unfortunately for the character, this modifier also applies to magical tests used for healing.

Cybermantic techniques also give a character an astral presence—the enchantments woven into his body shine like beacons on the astral plane. This has the same effect as if the character were constantly astrally perceiving—except that the character cannot actually see or sense astral space. The character has no awareness of astral space at all. Yes, this means the character can be attacked in astral space. Those are the breaks, chummer.

Karma Hazing

The term "karma hazing" was coined by a specific hermetic organization whose members apparently know more about this phenomenon than anyone else. They call it karma hazing because they believe that individuals with sub-zero Essence generate permanent astral pollution that may prove disastrous for the collective Karma of (meta)humanity.

Karma hazing makes the cybermantic character's astral presence increasingly noticeable to astrally active individuals and creatures, who can sense it far beyond normal ranges for assensing or astral awareness. Increasingly, the character's astral presence registers as a black shadow, a polluted zone. To all who can sense it, it somehow feels *wrong*. Astrally active creatures and individuals either shun the affected character or take hostile action against him, and astral predators may be drawn to his vicinity. Wraiths (p.110, **Paranormal Animals of Europe**) seem particularly sensitive to karma-hazed individuals.

The gamemaster may approach karma hazing in several ways. Most simply, he may ignore it—after all, the risks of dissociation and cancer caused by cybermancy are bad enough. Also, any megacorp that authorizes cybermancy for a character will protect their investment by ensuring that their mages do their damnedest to disguise the astral signature of a cybermantically sustained character.

Alternatively, the gamemaster may make a periodic Essence (4) Test for the character—every month or so, say, or during a run—treating the character's Essence Rating as positive for the purposes of the test (round fractions up). If the gamemaster achieves any successes, sooner or later *something* takes an active and hostile interest in the character. This something may be a critter wandering around the astral or a much more dangerous entity with a much more specific purpose. This hostile attention can form the basis for an entire adventure in which the character must shake off the astral menace.

CHANGES TO REACTION/PERCEPTION

For every point of negative Essence or part thereof that a character has, he receives a +1 modifier to all Reaction Tests made when he is taken by surprise (see **Surprise**, p. 86, **SRII**). For example, a character with an Essence Rating –1.3 would receive a +2 modifier to his Reaction Tests in these circumstances.

Additionally, a character receives a +2 modifier to all Perception Tests for every point of negative Essence or part thereof. In situations where a character is deliberately searching for or expecting something, he can reduce the Perception Test modifier by making a Willpower Test against a target number equal to three times the absolute value of his Essence Rating (round up). Each success from this test reduces the Perception Test modifier by 1.

Lost in the Details

Sometimes a cybermantically sustained character can get lost in the details of what he is observing. Whenever a character achieves all successes on Perception Tests with modified Target Numbers of 5 or more, this occurs. To break free, the character may immediately make a Willpower Test against the target number of the Perception Test. If the Willpower Test fails, the character remains lost in concentration.

The player may repeat the Willpower Test in every following Combat Turn or once per minute if not in combat. The target number increases by 1 each time the test is repeated. If the player fails 5 tests in a row, his invoked memory stimulator kicks in and the target number begins to drop by 1 per each Combat Turn or minute, whichever is more frequent.

Other characters may attempt to attract the cybermantic character's attention as well. Each such attempt reduces the Willpower Test target number by 1. During Combat Turns, characters must spend Simple Actions to make these attempts.

CHANGES TO WILLPOWER

For every half point of negative Essence or part thereof that a character has, his Willpower Rating is reduced by 1. A character with an Essence Rating of –.75, for example, would experience a Willpower Rating reduction of 2.

However, the cybermantic process magically restores up to 4 points of Willpower lost because of negative Essence. Note that cybermantic magic cannot increase the character's Willpower beyond the rating he possessed before undergoing cybermancy.

The character is also immune to any form of magic that can increase his Willpower Attribute, such as the Increase Attribute spell. Additionally, the cybermantic Willpower increase cannot be dispelled or broken and is not affected if magic is grounded into the character's body from astral space.

INVOKED MEMORY STIMULATOR

Whenever a cybermantically sustained character's invoked memory stimulator (IMS) kicks in, it dredges up various of the character's memories to keep him from slipping away. The character hears voices, sees faces, remembers people long dead or long forgotten, remembers good times and terrible times. The IMS and the memories it provokes have no specific game effects, but the gamemaster should use invoked memories as a roleplaying or storytelling tool. On occasion the character may even confuse memory with reality, and the gamemaster should feel free to mix and match reality with various memories as seems appropriate. However, keep in mind that this kind of confusion does not occur very often.

SOCIAL AND KARMA PENALTIES

A sub-zero Essence Rating causes characters to act strangely in social situations. To reflect this side effect, add the absolute value of the character's Essence Rating to the target numbers for all the character's Charisma and social-skill based tests (round fractions up). For Essence Ratings below –2, double the penalty for the amount below –2.

For example, a character with an Essence Rating of –3 receives a +4 modifier to appropriate target numbers: 2 for the first 2 points of negative Essence, plus 2 for the remaining point (1 x 2 = 2). A character with an Essence Rating of –3.5 receives a +5 modifier: 2 for the first 2 points of negative Essence, plus 3 for the remaining 1.5 points (1.5 x 2 = 3).

These penalties apply even if a strong emotional bond once existed between the character and the individual he is interacting with. Gamemasters may increase the penalties in such circumstances, because people who once knew the character well may be especially disconcerted by his strange behavior.

Cybermantic characters cannot compensate for their loss of social skills by any magical means. The character has crossed an absolute threshold, and anyone who meets him knows this at a gut, heart, and brain level.

These social modifiers do not apply in situations where the character intentionally intimidates others, such as an interrogation. In fact, the gamemaster may even use the character's Essence Rating to reduce the target numbers of tests in such situations.

Sub-zero Essence also reduces a character's ability to accumulate and use Karma. Such characters gain Karma at one-half the usual rate (p. 190, **SRII**). Additionally, characters cannot regain lost Essence by spending Good Karma.

LONG-TERM EFFECTS

Cybermantic treatments also may produce long-term side effects that may not be immediately apparent. These effects include chronic dissociation syndrome and cancer. (Hey, chummer, you're the one who wanted to be a walking dead guy. Deal with it.)

CHRONIC DISSOCIATION SYNDROME

Chronic dissociation syndrome (CDS) occurs when a character's response to his invoked memory stimulator (IMS) deteriorates. The IMS continues to provoke memories in the character's mind, but he ceases to respond to them in the same way. Instead, he experiences the memories as alien to himself. The memories produce the same disruptive effects described in **Invoked Memory Stimulator** and they gradually lose their power to "anchor" the character to the real world as well. The images that occupy him are devoid of meaning, a jumble of disconnected events and appearances that serve only to confuse and painfully remind the character of the life he once had. The character loses the will to live and seems to fade away from the land of the living, his last days spent in a soulless catatonic state.

CHRONIC DISSOCIATION SYNDROME TABLE

Essence Rating	Frequency of Tests	Target Number
–0.05 to –0.50	1 every 6 months	3
–0.55 to –1.00	1 every 6 months	4
–1.05 to –1.50	1 every 6 months	5
–1.55 to –2.00	1 every 4 months	5
–2.05 to –2.50	1 every 4 months	6
–2.55 to –3.00	1 every 3 months	6
–3.05 to –3.50	1 every 2 months	6
–3.55 or lower	1 every 2 months	8; +1 to target number for every additional –0.5

The gamemaster makes periodic Willpower Tests to determine whether a character develops CDS. The frequency and target number for the tests are determined by the character's Essence Rating as shown on the Chronic Dissociation Syndrome Table. Willpower modifiers from cybermantic magic apply to this test, but similar modifiers from any other shorter-term magical source do not.

If a Willpower Test fails, CDS has set in and the character is lost to the world. He cannot initiate action, only react. For example, the character cannot initiate combat but can defend himself against attacks. CDS adds a +4 modifiers to all Perception Tests the character makes and a +3 modifier for all other tests. Note that these modifiers are in addition to any other modifiers already applied to the character's tests.

The character sickens, will not eat, develops untreatable insomnia and dies in a number of weeks equal to 3 + his Willpower Rating.

Chronic dissociation syndrome is treatable magically, but only trained magicians—those capable of performing the original cybermantic rituals—can perform the treatment. (They don't teach the tricks of the trade either, for damned good reasons.) Assuming the treatment is conducted in a delta clinic, the afflicted character makes a Spell Resistance (8) Test. If the test succeeds, the magic fails and the character dies. If the Spell Resistance Test fails, the syndrome is reversed and the character's IMS begins to function effectively, though it takes a few days for this to happen. The character makes a Willpower (6) Test to determine how quickly this recovery occurs. The base time for this recovery is 1 week; each success on the Willpower Test shortens the recovery time by 1 day.

CDS treatment becomes increasingly difficult each time the syndrome sets in, so reduce the target number for the Spell Resistance Test by 1 each time a character repeats the test. The target number may never drop below 2, however.

CANCER

Cybermancy produces an artificial, forced alliance between a character's body and spirit. Magical and technological trickery is used to "fool" the spirit into staying, but this means that the body as well as the spirit develops problems.

Just as the insidious sickness of the spirit manifests as karma hazing, the body's sickness manifests as cancer. At a very deep, primal level, the body *knows* that the spirit is not truly present in it. As a result, the P46–gatekeeper/MIC gene systems present in every (meta)human, which normally instruct body cells to die in a pre-programmed fashion, no longer send the right biochemical signals. Cells that should die remain alive and become cancerous. At the same time, cells that should stay alive die, and the body necrotizes. This is a ghastly end.

To determine whether the character will suffer this particular long-term effect, roll 2D6 during the initial cybermantic operation. If the result is less than double the absolute value of the character's intended Essence Rating, the character will eventually develop cancer (if he lives long enough). At the gamemaster's discretion, the roll result may be increased by 1 if the character's unaugmented Body Rating is between 4 and 7, and by 2 if the Body Rating is 8 or better—high Body Ratings reduce the chances of cancer developing. If the individual has circulating symbiotes (p. 15, **Shadowtech**), the dice roll result can be increased by 1 at the gamemaster's discretion.

If the test fails, the character will develop cancer after 10D6 months. The cancer will be fast-growing, extremely nasty, and incurable. It will kill kill the character within 5 to 10 weeks of its appearance (4 + 1D6). The gamemaster decides when to inform the player of his character's condition.

CYBERMANTIC MAGIC

This book provides no rules for the spells, rituals and magical operations involved in cybermancy simply because shadowrunners are never going to be able to use them. Even if by some wild stretch of the imagination a player character managed to learn cybermantic techniques, the knowledge would be worth nothing unless he also had access to a delta clinic and a dedicated medical staff at his beck and call for weeks on end (which isn't going to happen).

The **Magic and Death** section indicates the tasks involved in cybermantic magic. The ritual requires a dedicated group, takes at least 24 hours to accomplish, involves the equivalent of an astral quest (though nowhere near as difficult as the usual kind, unless the subject of the magical treatment is intended to end up with a *very* low Essence), and also involves powerful spirits in some way. Usually these are Spirits of Man, though a certain organization has learned to employ blood spirits instead. Finally, some extended form of metamagical centering is used to focus the spirit of the subject to enhance the magical "anchoring" of that spirit to the body.

The drain produced by the ritual is stupefying—players and gamemasters shouldn't even want to think about the number of dice rolls that would be needed to simulate it (and all those double-digit Damage codes get really depressing after a while). Even high-level initiates of a hermetic group, who can use extra-effective Centering techniques against Drain, think more than twice about it when they're preparing for the ritual.

Only a small number of hermetic organizations know the rituals necessary for cybermantic magic. They are not owners or major shakers in corporations, but they willingly work for corporate interests and instruct a few corporate mages in just enough of the techniques to enable them to perform cybermancy. They do not teach the corp mages quite enough to pull off the really heavy-duty stuff, such as taking Essence below –3. And these organizations only teach those corporate mages who have donated blood, skin, bonded foci and similar elements of their magical selves as assurances of their good behavior, to ensure that the students will never pose a threat to their instructors. They make sure that when it comes to the really big numbers, they must be called in personally. And their fees are high enough to buy a Fairlight with the change.

Magic and Death gives some hints on why these organizations do this. Money is one obvious motive, but big-time hermetics are rarely motivated by greed alone. To some extent, the power gained by becoming a big-gun cybermancer motivates some. Of course, these organizations may have far more important motives.

If a player thinks about having his character hit that delta clinic, don't let him forget into whose hands he might be putting himself. Let him worry a little about it before he makes his choice, because once he's gone through with the treatment, worrying won't do him any good.

CHROME KINGS

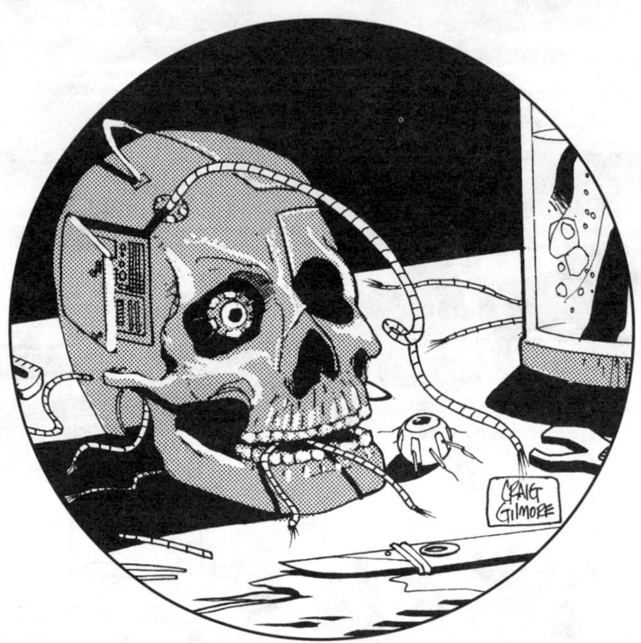

The following fully chromed **Shadowrun** characters can be used as contacts or NPCs. They use a mix of alpha-, beta-, and delta-grade cyberware and gear from this book and from **SRII**, the **Street Samurai Catalog**, **Shadowtech**, and **Fields of Fire**. These characters are not archetypes and should not be used as starting characters (unless the gamemaster is into high-octane masochism).

As suggested in **Shadowtech,** gamemasters may decide to gradually introduce into their game the equipment and concepts described in this book in order to fully explore how these issues will affect game balance. Treat the chrome kings provided in this section as active or former runners who have chosen a specific lifestyle, one from which there is no turning back. Cybermancy is the ultimate destination on the cybertech road, and it is still a pretty scary place. Players should be made to understand that the experimental nature of cybermancy offers no guarantees. Those who accept cybermancy are literally putting their lives into someone else's hands—no easy thing for a general class of people who may be kindly described as control freaks. They know who they are going in, but will they still be someone after their next piece of cyberware?

CYBER RUNNER

"Riding on the cutting edge isn't everything, chummers. You can run like the wind to keep up with the state-of-the-art cybertech designs, but no matter how fast you run there's always gonna be some slot somewhere who's gonna have newer toys than you. That's just the way it is. Spend all the nuyen you want—that old cutting edge is always gonna be just beyond your reach. Of course, no one says you have to keep running a race that you're never gonna win.

"Remember, all the chrome in the world is no match for brains—and all the nuyen in the world can't buy that. I've seen too many runners who get chromed to the teeth and fall so in love with their new goodies that they forget to use the one thing that's kept them alive—their brains.

"The choice is yours. You can go the chromehead route or you can play it smart. It really doesn't matter to me."

Commentary

The cyber runner is a veteran of the streets. He packs some serious cyberware, but he owes his success to his smarts—and he knows it. Anyone who asks him gets the same advice—flexibility and intelligence will always win out over raw firepower and two tons of chrome. The cyber runner can handle himself in any situation and often acts as a mentor to promising up-and-coming street sams.

Attributes
Body: 7
Quickness: 4
Strength: 4
Charisma: 5
Intelligence: 4
Willpower: 4
Essence: 0.55
Reaction: 4 (13)

Skills
Armed Combat: 6
Athletics: 6
Bike: 4
Biotech: 3
Etiquette (Street): 4
Firearms: 7
Gunnery: 5
Stealth: 5
Unarmed Combat (Cyberweapon): 7

Initiative: 4 (13) + 1D6 (3D6)
Body Index: 2.1
Threat/Professional Rating: 5/4

Bioware
Damage Compensator (3)
Enhanced Articulation
Synthacardium (2)
Tailored Pheromones (2)

Cyberware
Balance Augmentor
Bone Lacing (Plastic)
Cybereyes (Low-Light, Rangefinder, Thermographic)
Hand Blade (Retractable)
Reaction Enhancer (+4)
Smartlink II
Wired Reflexes (2) (alpha)

Gear
Ares Crusader MP (w/200 rounds explosive ammo, Level II Smartlink, Improved Gas Vent II)
Armor Jacket
Franchi SPAS-22 (w/80 rounds explosive ammo, Level II Smartlink, Improved Gas Vent III)
Survival Knife
Walther Palm Pistol (w/6 rounds APDS ammo)
Additional gear as appropriate

SPECIAL FORCES TROOPER

"Listen—I'm tired, we're all tired of the megacorps and their hardboys underestimating the power of the Federal government. Some nuyen-grubbing suits put a coupla million nuyen worth of hardware into a slag and they think the guy's some kinda super-fraggin'-cyberboy. They assemble a few of these freaks in their little labs and they think they got an army.

"Then they sit around in their little boardrooms and congratulate each other on how rich and powerful they are. They tell each other they're fraggin' geniuses and sit around grinning, smugly confident that their drek don't stink like everyone else's. 'Why no Hal, yours don't smell. How 'bout mine?' They think they can call the shots and do whatever the hell they want.

"Well some day—maybe sooner than they think—we're going to have it out with one of them uppity megacorps. They'll get a little taste of what it's like to rock and roll with a *real* army. Then we'll see who's boss."

Commentary

The special forces trooper may belong to the military of virtually any country in the world. Cybered and ready for action, he'll go anywhere and do anything for his country. He's fiercely proud of his skills and abilities, as well as his unit. Like a rapidly growing number of other military men, he resents the privileged personnel who populate the private armies of the megacorps and relishes any opportunity to go up against them.

Attributes
Body: 5 (6)
Quickness: 6
Strength: 5
Charisma: 3
Intelligence: 4
Willpower: 4
Essence: 0.38
Reaction: 5 (9)

Skills
Armed Combat: 4
Athletics: 3
Firearms: 5
Gunnery: 4
Stealth: 4
Tactics (Small Unit): 3
Unarmed Combat: 4

Initiative: 5 (9) + 1D6 (2D6)
Body Index: .6
Threat/Professional Rating: 4/3

Bioware
Pain Editor

Cyberware
Commlink IV
Crypto-Circuit HD (5)
Cybercomm Link
Cyberears (Hearing Amplification, Spatial Recognizer)
Cybereyes (Low-Light, Rangefinder, Laser Designator)
Dermal Sheath (2) (alpha)*
Reaction Enhancer (+2)
Smartlink II
Wired Reflexes (1) (alpha)

Gear
Ares Alpha Combat Gun (w/168 rounds APDS ammo, 8 IPE offensive grenades, Level II Smartlink, Improved Gas Vent II)
Colt Manhunter (w/48 rounds APDS ammo, Level II Smartlink)
Fineblade Knife (long blade)
Medium Military Armor (w/helmet)
Additional gear as appropriate

*Impact Armor +1

CYBER ASSASSIN

>>>>CLASSIFIED<<<<<

>>>>NO DATA AVAILABLE<<<<<

Attributes
Body: 4 (5)
Quickness: 5 (7)
Strength: 5
Charisma: 3
Intelligence: 4
Willpower: 5
Essence: 0.16
Reaction: 5 (9)

Skills
Armed Combat: 4
Athletics: 3
Bike: 4
Biotech: 4
Car: 4
Computer: 4
Demolitions: 5
Etiquette (Corporate): 4
Etiquette (Street): 4
Firearms: 8
Interrogation: 5
Physical Sciences: 3
Psychology: 3
Rotorcraft: 4
Stealth: 8
Throwing: 4
Unarmed Combat: 7
Winged Planes: 4

Initiative: 5 (9) + 1D6 (3D6)
Body Index: 4.0
Threat/Professional Rating: 6/4

Bioware
Adrenal Pump (2)
Pain Editor
Synthacardium (2)
Toxin Exhaler

Cyberware
Air Filter (5)
Blood Filter (5) (alpha)
Bone Lacing (Plastic) (alpha)
Cranial Area Bomb (set to detonate upon death
Cyberears [Balance Augmentor (alpha), Hearing Amplification, Select Sound Filter (3), Sound Damper]
Cybereyes (alpha) (Datajack, Flare Compensation, Low-Light, Thermographic, Optical Scanning Retinal Clock, Rangefinder, Tool Laser) (all alpha)
Internal Air Tank
Move-By-Wire System (2) (beta)

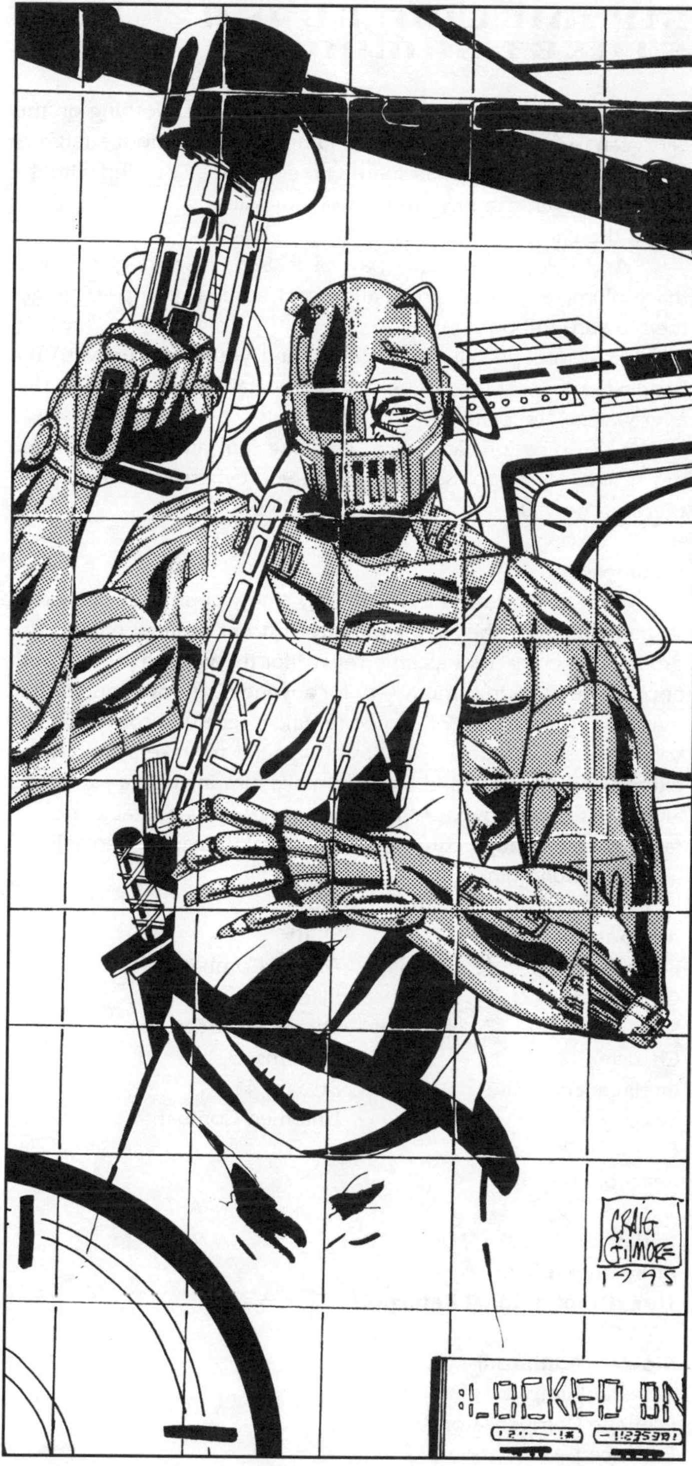

Gear
Barret Model 121 [w/28 rounds APDS ammo, Sound Suppressor, Bipod, Level II Smartlink, Imaging Scope (Low-Light, Mag 3), Ruthenium Polymer Case w/6 Imaging Scanners]
Ceska vz/120 (54 round APDS ammo, Silencer, Level II Smartlink)
Morrissey Elan (10 rounds APDS ammo)
Ruthenium Polymer Armored Suit (Armor 5/2, 6 Imaging Scanners)
Shock Glove
Shuriken (6, w/Dikote™ edge)
Survival Knife (w/Dikote™ edge)
Additional gear as appropriate

SIX MILLION NUYEN STREET SAMURAI

"The world has never seen anything like me. Nothing on this earth can move faster, see farther, jump higher, or shoot straighter than me. My employer has spared no expense—I'm filled with the best that nuyen can buy. You could work all your life and still not afford the chrome inside my right arm alone.

"And cyberware's only part of it. Suprathyroid gland, synthacardium, enhanced articulation and adrenal pump—I've got the bioware to boot.

"Now you put all this together and you come up with the baddest, meanest, most un-fraggin'-beatable cybermaniac that ever walked the planet.

"I can dice 'em and slice 'em, frag 'em and scrag 'em and never lose my edge. So look out all you cyberslags out there—there's a new kid in town."

Commentary

With the advent of cybermancy, a new class of street samurai has emerged. The six million nuyen street samurai typifies this group. This character has little regard for the wisdom and experience of the veteran samurai—or for anyone else's opinion, for that matter. A classic case of someone who's received too much too soon, the six million nuyen street samurai mistakenly thinks his extensive cyberware and bioware make him invincible—and he's all too eager to prove it. While he may not be unbeatable, he certainly carries enough chrome to be a lethal menace to himself and anyone around him.

Attributes
Body: 6 (9)
Quickness: 4 (7)
Strength: 6 (9)
Charisma: 2
Intelligence: 5
Willpower: 5
Essence: -7.6 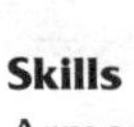
Reaction: 6 (13)

Skills
Armed Combat: 4
Bike: 3
Etiquette (Street): 3
Firearms: 5
Stealth: 4
Unarmed Combat: 4

Initiative: 6 (13) + 1D6 (+ 4D6)
Body Index: 5.25
Threat/Professional Rating: 4/4

Bioware (cultured)
Adrenal Pump (2)
Damage Compensator 3
Enhanced Articulation
Orthoskin 3
Suprathyroid Gland
Synthacardium (2)

Cyberware
Blood Filter (2) (beta)
Cybereyes (beta) (Flare Compensation, Low-Light, Thermographic)
Muscle Replacement 2 (beta)
Retractable Spur (beta)
Smartlink II (2) (beta)
Wired Reflexes (3) (beta)
Invoked Memory Stimulator (delta)
Dermal Sheath 2 (delta)

Gear
Ares Predator II (w/45 rounds regular ammo, Level II Smartlink)
Armor Jacket
DocWagon™ Contract (Platinum)
Uzi-III (w/100 rounds regular ammo, Level II Smartlink, Gas Vent III)
Additional gear as appropriate

CYBERZOMBIE

"Regrets? Your question shows how little you know, how little you understand.

"I am more than I ever could have been—far more than you can ever hope to be. I have no reason for regrets. I have lost nothing and gained everything. Nothing can stop me now. Nothing.

"It is true that I no longer enjoy the easy camaraderie that I once shared with my former companions. But I do not miss that. I have no time for sentimentality. Such niceties can only confuse the mind and slow the reflexes. Only misguided weaklings feel the need for such luxuries.

"Understand that I no longer live in the world of human weaknesses and foibles. I am the first of a new breed, the man of the future. Do not be ashamed of your fear and resentment. It is only natural that you should feel such things in the presence of your evolutionary successor."

Commentary

The cyberzombie is a delta-grade cybersoldier. Combine an unlimited budget, the latest cyberware, and the finest design teams available and he's what you get. Of course, even the best designers can't always accurately predict what's going to happen when you take those elegant plans on the drawing board and bring them to life. Sure, the cyberzombie's not the most friendly or coherent guy in the world—but that doesn't mean you should be afraid of him. Does it?

Of course, the big question remains: Is he still human? Do you want to ask him?

Attributes
Body: 4 (11)
Quickness: 4 (7)
Strength: 6 (9)
Charisma: 2
Intelligence: 5
Willpower: 5
Essence: –2.25
Reaction: 6 (13)

Skills
Armed Combat: 7
Athletics: 6
Firearms: 8
Gunnery: 6
Stealth: 6
Tactics (Small Unit): 5
Unarmed Combat: 8

Initiative: 4 (10) + 1D6 (4D6)
Body Index: 0
Threat/Professional Rating: 9/4

Cyberware (all delta grade)
Articulate Arm
Body Plating (Hardened; 8/8)
Cyberarms (left/right: Strength +3, Quickness +3, Body +2, Cyberlimb Magnetic System, Gyromount)
Cyberears (Balance Augmentor, Damper, Hearing Amplification, Spatial Recognizer,)
Cybereyes (Electronic Vision Magnification 3, Eye Light, Flare Compensation, Laser Tracker, Low-Light, Thermographic, Protective Covers, Rangefinder)
Cyberlegs (right/left; Strength +4, Quickness +3, Body +2, Cyberlimb Magnetic System, Foot Anchor)
Cyberskull
Cybertorso
Internal Air Tank
Move-By-Wire System (2)
Oral Spur
Smartlink II
Invoked Memory Stimulator

Gear
Ares Alpha Combat Guns (2, each w/300 rounds APDS ammo, Level II Smartlink, Improved Gas Vent III, 8 IPE offensive and 8 IPE defensive grenades)
Ares MP-LMG (300 rounds APDS ammo, Laser Tracker, Improved Gas Vent III)
Additional gear as appropriate

CYBER LOGICIAN

"I always make the correct tactical decision, because emotion does not cloud my judgment. My mental processes are unaffected by fear, compassion, sentimentality—any of the troublesome feelings that may afflict an unaugmented commander.

"I do whatever is necessary to attain my client's designated objective in the most effective manner possible, while minimizing the loss of the client's resources. Collateral damage is irrelevant.

"I have no affection for heroics or showmanship, and I do not tolerate such wasteful sentiments among my team members."

Commentary

The cyber logician is a master of small-unit tactics, the ultimate tactical commander. Already certain megacorporations employ cyber logicians for field work in particularly sensitive areas, and the high success rates achieved by these individuals ensure their use will increase in the future. If you and your kind get uppity, chummer, you may well end up meeting one of these chromed commanders. They usually give the orders, but any cybered logician is perfectly capable of dealing with you personally if necessary.

Attributes	**Skills**	
Body: 4 (10)	Armed Combat: 6	Psychology
Quickness: 4 (8)	Computer: 8	(Deviant Behavior): 6
Strength: 3 (7)	Computer Theory: 7	(Group Behavior): 7
Charisma: 3	Electronics: 5	Unarmed Combat: 6
Intelligence: 5 (7)	Firearms: 6	
Willpower: 4	Interrogation: 7	
Essence: –4.0	Military Theory: 5	
Reaction: 3 (8)	Leadership: 8	

Initiative: 4 (Special) + 1D6 (4D6)
Body Index: 1.2
Threat/Professional Rating: 9/4

Bioware (cultured)
Cerebral Booster (Level II)
Mnemonic Enhancer (Level IV)

Cyberware (all delta)
Commlink IV
Crypto Circuit 10
Cyberarms (left/right: Strength +4, Quickness +6, Body +2)
    Cyberlimb Cyberdeck (MPCP 8, Hardening +6, Persona 8, Increased Response +3, Internal
    Memory 1,200 Mp0
    Fingertip Compartment
    Fingertip Datajack
    Tactical Computer (Level 4, w.Orientaion System)
Cybercomm Link
Cyberears (High- and Low- Frequency, Recorder)
Cybereyes (Camera, Eye Light System w/BrightLight, Low-Light, Rangefinder, Thermographic Flare Compensation)
Cyberskull
Datajack (Head)
Invoked Memory Stimulator
Skillwire (Small-Unit Tactics, Rating 9)
Smartlink II
Subdermal Speakers
Subvocal Microphones

Gear
Ares Alpha Combat Guns (2, w/300 rounds APDS ammo, Level II Smartlink, Improved Gas Vent III, 8 IPE offensive and 8 IPE defensive grenades)
Ares MP-LMG (w/300 rounds APDS ammo, Laser Tracker, Improved Gas Vent III)
Wallacher Combat Axes (2)
Additional gear as appropriate

CYBERTECHNOLOGY TABLE

NOTE: This table includes cyberware from Cybertechnology and all previously published Shadowrun products.

HEADWARE

	Essence Cost	Cost	Availability	Street Index	Legality
Chemical Analyzer	.2	2,500¥/level	4/6 days	1	Legal
Chipjack	.2	1,000¥	3/72 hrs	.9	Legal
Cranial Bombs					
Kink Bomb	—	28,000¥	12/14 days	1.5	2-CC
Microbomb	—	65,500¥	18/48 hrs	1.25	2-CC
Area Bomb	—	500,000¥	20/14 days	1	2-CC
Data Filter	.3	5,000¥	6/36 hrs	1.5	Legal
Datajack (**SR** rules)	.2	1,000¥	Always	.9	Legal
Datajack (**Shadowtech**)					
Level 1	.1	500¥	Always	.9	Legal
Level 2	.15	1,000¥	Always	.9	Legal
Level 3	.2	2,000¥	Always	.9	Legal
Level 4	.25	4,000¥	Always	.9	Legal
Data Lock	.2	1,000¥	6/36 hrs	1.5	Legal
Datasoft Link	.1	1,000¥	3/24 hrs	1	Legal
Encephalon					
Level 1	.5	15,000¥	6/12 days	2	Legal
Level 2	.75	40,000¥	6/12 days	2	Legal
Level 3	1.5	75,000¥	6/12 days	2	Legal
Level 4	1.75	115,000¥	6/12 days	2	Legal
Gas Spectrometer	.2	2,000¥/level	4/5 days	1	Legal
Internal Voice Mask	.1	7,000¥	6/48 hrs	1	6-CA
Memory	Mp ÷ 100	Mp x 100¥	2/24 hrs	1	Legal
Memory (FIFF)	Mp ÷ 300	Mp x 150¥	3/24 hrs	.8	Legal
Olfactory Booster	.2	1,000¥/level	6/8 days	1	Legal
Orientation System	.5	15,000¥	5/6 days	1.5	Legal
Sense Link	2	300,000¥	2/5 days	1	10P-CA
Internal Transmitter	.6	80,000¥	3/5 days	1.5	8P-CA
Softlink (Level 1)	.15	1,000Y	3/72 hrs	.9	Legal
Level 2	.2	2,000¥	3/72 hrs	.9	Legal
Level 3	.25	4,000¥	3/72 hrs	.9	Legal
Level 4	.3	8,000¥	3/72 hrs	.9	Legal
SPU: Data Management					
Level 1	.1	9,500¥	6/60 hrs	1	Legal
Level 2	.15	19,000¥	6/60 hrs	1	Legal
Level 3	.2	28,500¥	6/60 hrs	1	Legal
Level 4	.25	38,000¥	6/60 hrs	1	Legal
SPU: Input/Output					
Level 1	.1	5,000¥	5/4 days	1.5	Legal
Level 2	.15	7,500¥	5/4 days	1.5	Legal
Level 3	.2	12,500¥	5/4 days	1.5	Legal
Level 4	.25	22,500¥	5/4 days	1.5	Legal
SPU: Math					
Level 1	.1	2,000¥	6/60 hrs	1	Legal
Level 2	.15	5,000¥	6/60 hrs	1	Legal
Level 3	.2	11,000¥	6/60 hrs	1	Legal
Level 4	.25	23,000¥	6/60 hrs	1	Legal
Tactical Computer					
Level 1	3.5	350,000¥	12/60 days	4	4-CB
Level 2	4	900,000¥	12/60 days	4	4-CC
Level 3–4	(See text)		CLASSIFIED		2-CC

HEADWARE

	Essence Cost	Cost	Availability	Street Index	Legality
Video Link	.5	22,000¥	4/48 hrs	1	Legal
Internal Transmitter	.4	4,500¥	6/48 hrs	1	Legal
Communications					
Commlink II	.3	8,000¥	2/48 hrs	1	Legal
Commlink IV	.3	18,000¥	3/48 hrs	1.25	Legal
Commlink VIII	.3	40,000¥	4/48 hrs	1.5	Legal
Commlink X	.3	60,000¥	5/48 hrs	1.75	Legal
Crypto Circuit HD					
Level 1–4	.1	Level x 10,000¥	6/36 hrs	1	4P-CA
Level 5–7	.1	Level x 20,000¥	6/36 hrs	1.25	4P-CA
Level 8–9	.1	Level x 30,000¥	8/36 hrs	1.5	3P-CA
Level 10	.1	500,000¥	9/36 hrs	2	3P-CA
Cybercomm Link	.4	62,000¥	8/2 weeks	3	5-CB
Radio	.75	4,000¥	2/24 hrs	.8	Legal
Radio Receiver	.4	2,000¥	2/24 hrs	.8	Legal
Scramble Breaker HD					
Level 1–4	.2	Level x 20,000¥	6/48 hrs	1.5	3-CB
Level 5–7	.2	Level x 40,000¥	8/48 hrs	1.75	3-CB
Level 8	.2	600,000¥	10/48 hrs	1.75	3-CB
Subdermal Speakers	.1	650¥	4/72 hrs	2	Legal
Subvocal Microphones					
External	—	500¥	3/48 hrs	1.25	Legal
Internal	.1	850¥	4/72 hrs	2	Legal
Telephone	.5	3,700¥	3/24 hrs	.9	Legal
Ears					
Balance Augmentor	.4	14,000¥	8/2 weeks	2	Legal
Cosmetic Modification	—	1,000¥	2/24 hrs	.8	Legal
Cyber Replacement	.3	4,000¥	2/24 hrs	.75	Legal
Damper	.1	3,500¥	4/48 hrs	1.25	Legal
Hearing Amplification	.2	3,500¥	4/48 hrs	1.25	Legal
High Frequency	.2	3,000¥	4/48 hrs	1.25	Legal
Low Frequency	.2	3,000¥	4/48 hrs	1.25	Legal
Modification	.1	2,000¥	2/24 hrs	1	Legal
Recorder	.3	7,000¥	8/48 hrs	2	12P-CA
Select Sound Filter (Levels 1–5)	.2	Level x 10,000¥	6/48 hrs	1.25	Legal
Spatial Recognizer	.2	1,200¥	4/48 hrs	2	Legal
Eyes					
Camera	.4	5,000¥	6/24 hrs	2	Legal
Cosmetic Modification	—	1,000¥	2/24 hrs	.75	Legal
Cyber Replacement	.2	5,000¥	2/24 hrs	.75	Legal
Display Link	.1	1,000¥	4/36 hrs	1	Legal
Dr. Spott Smartcam Implant	2	10,000¥	6/4 days	2	Legal
Eyecrafters Opticam Package	.5	20,000¥	5/72 hrs	2	Legal
Flare Compensation	.1	2,000¥	5/48 hrs	1.25	Legal
Image Link	.2	1,600¥	4/48 hrs	2	Legal
Low-Light	.2	3,000¥	4/36 hrs	1.25	Legal
Protective Covers	—	500¥	4/48 hrs	1.5	Legal
Rangefinder	.1	2,000¥	8/48 hrs	1.5	Legal
Retinal Clock	.1	450¥	3/24 hrs	1	Legal
Retinal Duplication (illegal)	.1	50,000¥+	12/7 days	2	3-CA
Thermographic	.2	3,000¥	4/36 hrs	1.25	Legal
Vision Magnification					
Optical 1	.2	2,500¥	4/48 hrs	1	Legal
Optical 2	.2	4,000¥	4/48 hrs	1	Legal

HEADWARE

	Essence Cost	Cost	Availability	Street Index	Legality
Optical 3	.2	6,000¥	5/48 hrs	1	Legal
Electronic 1	.1	3,500¥	5/48 hrs	1	Legal
Electronic 2	.1	7,500¥	5/48 hrs	1	Legal
Electronic 3	.1	11,000¥	8/48 hrs	1	Legal
Eye Datajacks					
Eye Dataport	.25	2,200¥	6/48 hrs	2	4U-CD
Optical Scanning Datajack	.3	5,500¥	8/72 hrs	3	3U-CD
Optical Scanning Datajack					
Emitter (Concealability 10)	—	8/2 weeks	2,500¥	2	3U-CD
Eye Laser Systems					
Laser Designator (range 4,000 m)	.5	12,000¥	12/1 month	3	5P-CC
Laser Tracker (range 400 m)	.2	3,200¥	8/72 hrs	2	4P-CC
Tool Laser (range 4 m)	.25	5,200¥	8/1 week	2	Legal
Eye Light Systems					
Eye Light Systems	.2	1,200¥	4/72 hrs	1.5	Legal
BrightLight Addition	.4	1,200¥	8/2 weeks	3	7I-CB
w/ Flash-pak	—	+1,000¥	8/2 weeks	3	7I-CB
each One Shot Flash-pak	—	+500¥	8/2 weeks	3	7I-CB
Eye Weapons					
Eye Dart	.25	4,200¥	8/2 weeks	2	7P-CC
Eye Gun	.4	6,400¥	6/1 week	3	7P-CC
Oral Weapons					
Oral Dart	.25	3,600¥	6/1 weeks	2	6P-CC
Oral Gun	.4	5,600¥	6/72 hrs	3	6P-CC
Oral Spur	.25	8,200¥	6/72 hrs	2.5	6P-CC
Oral Whip	.25	10,500¥	8/1 week	2.5	6P-CC
Tooth Compartment					
Tooth Compartment					
Breakable	—	700¥	3/48 hrs	1.5	10P-CB
Storage	—	1,500¥	2/48 hrs	1.25	Legal

MATRIXWARE

	Essence Cost	Cost	Availability	Street Index	Legality
Hardening	.3	See **Shadowtech**	Varies/8 days	Varies	4-CD
Memory/Storage	Mp ÷ 300	Mp x 150¥	3/24 hrs	.8	Legal
MPCP	(Rating/10) + .1	(Rating^3) x 200¥	12/60 days	4	4-CD
Persona Module	.3	See **Shadowtech**	Varies/12 days	Varies	4-CD
Response	.2	See **Shadowtech**	Varies/14 days	Varies	4-CD
Transfer	.1	See **Shadowtech**	Varies/10 days	Varies	4-CD

BODYWARE

	Essence Cost	Cost	Availability	Street Index	Legality
Automatic-Medication System	—	15,000¥/refill	NA	NA	NA 3P-CC
Body Plating					
Soft Armor	—	10,000¥/level	12/2 weeks	2	6P-CA
Hard Armor	—	25,000¥/level	14/3 weeks	2	5P-CA
Bone Lacing					
Plastic	.5	7,500¥	5/14 days	1.5	6P-CA
Aluminum	1.15	25,000¥	5/14 days	1.5	6P-CB
Titanium	2.25	75,000¥	5/14 days	1.5	6-CC
Cybertorso	1.5	120,000¥	6/4 days	1	Legal
Cyberskull	.75	75,000¥	6/4 days	1	Legal
CyberSquirt	—	1,400¥	8/6 days	2	4P-CC
Fingertip Compartment	.1	3,000¥	3/24 hrs	1	Legal
Fingertip Datajack		Per standard datajack			
Fingertip ExpertPicks	—	18,000¥	8/2 weeks	3	6P-CC

BODYWARE

	Essence Cost	Cost	Availability	Street Index	Legality
Fingertip Needle	—	800¥	4/72 hrs	1.5	6P-CB
Hand Blade	.1	7,500¥	6/5 days	1.5	4P-CC
Retractable	.25	10,000¥	6/5 days	1.5	3P-CC
Hand Razors	.1	4,500¥	3/72 hrs	1	3-B
Hydraulic Jack					
(Levels1–6)	.25	Level x 5,000¥	5/6 days	1	Legal
Induction Datajack	.3	3,000¥	5/4 days	2	Legal
Invoked Memory Stimulator	.25	137,750¥	NA	NA	3P-CC
Internal Air Tank	.25	1,200¥	4/5 days	1.5	Legal
Muscle Replacement					
(Maximum Rating 4)	Rating	Rating x 20,000¥	4/4 days	1	5P-CB
Retractable Razors	.2	9,000¥	5/72 hrs	1	3-B
Retractable Spur	.3	11,500¥	5/72 hrs	1	3-B
Shock Hand	—	1,300¥	6/4 days	2	4P-CC
Smartcam Link	.5	2,500¥	4/48 hrs	2	Legal
Smartlink (Lvl I)	.5	2,500¥	3/36 hrs	1	5P-CA
Smartlink (Lvl II)	.5	3,200¥	6/48 hrs	2	5P-CA

BODYWARE

	Essence Cost	Cost	Availability	Street Index	Legality
Spur	.1	7,000¥	3/72 hrs	1	3-B
Voice Modulator	.2	45,000¥	2/24 hrs	1	Legal
Increased Volume	—	10,000¥	2/24 hrs	1	Legal
Playback	.2	40,000¥	4/48 hrs	1	Legal
Secondary Pattern	—	50,000¥	6/7 days	2	Legal
Tonal Shift	—	25,000¥	2/24 hrs	1	Legal
Limbs					
Built-In Device	—	4 x Normal Cost	Varies	Varies	Varies
Built-In Smartgun Link	.25	2,500¥	6/4 days	1.5	5P-CA
Cyberarm Gyromount	1.5	260,000¥	10/21 days	2	4P-CC
Direct Neural Interface	.1	4,500¥	4/6 days	1	5P-CC
Cyberarm Cyberdeck	—	See text	See text	NA	6P-CD
Cyberarm Taser	—	2,000¥	6/4 days	1.5	5P-CC
Cyber Guns					
Hold-Out Pistol	—	250¥	8/7 days	2	8P-CB + E
Light Pistol	—	650¥	8/7 days	2	6P-CB + E
Machine Pistol	—	900¥	8/7 days	2	4-CB + G
Submachine Gun	—	1,800¥	8/7 days	2	3-CB + G
Heavy Pistol	—	800¥	8/7 days	2	4P-CB + E
Shotgun	—	1,200¥	8/7 days	2	4P-CB + E
Cyber Limbs					
Cyberarm/Leg	1	100,000¥	4/4 days	1	Legal
Cyberhand/Foot	.35	45,000¥	3/4 days	1	Legal
Cyber Forearm/Lower Leg	.65	70,000¥	4/4 days	1	Legal
Semi-natural Covering	—	+10%	Same as limb	1	Legal
Foot Anchor	.4	14,000¥	6/7 days	2	Legal
Increased Strength	—	Level x 150,000¥	6/4 days	1.5	6P-CA
Magnetic Cyberlimb System					
(per cyberlimb)	—	2,800¥	6/7 days	2	Legal
Replacement Hand	—	28,000¥	12/14 days	2	6I-CA
Simple Replacement	1	50,000¥	4/48 hrs	1	Legal
Limb Enhancements					
Body Enhancement	—	75,000¥/point	6/4 days	1.5	6P-CB
Quickness Enhancement					
1–3 points (per limb)	—	90,000¥/point	8/4 days	1.5	6P-CB
4+ points (per limb)	.3/point	110,000¥/point	8/4 days	1.5	6P-CB
Strength Enhancement					
1–3 points (per limb)	—	150,000¥/point	6/4 days	1.5	6P-CB
4+ points (per limb)	.4/point	175,000¥/point	6/4 days	1.5	6P-CB
Move-by-Wire System					
Level 1	2.5	250,000¥	8/10 days	2.5	3P-CC
Level 2	3.85	500,000¥	12/20 days	3	3P-CC
Level 3	5.2	1,250,000¥	18/30 days	3	3P-CC
Level 4	6.45	3,000,000¥	20/45 days	3.5	3P-CC
Simrigs					
Baseline Cyberware Simrig	2	300,000¥	8/12 days	3	Legal
Full-X Cyberware Simrig	2	500,000¥	6/12 days	3	Legal
Baseline Induction Simrig	2	50,000¥	6/4 days	2	Legal
Simlinks					
Internal (Rating 1–10)	.6 + (Rating x .05)	70k¥ + (10k¥ x Rating)	8/7 days	3	Legal
Boosted Reflexes					
Level 1	.5	15,000¥	3/24 hrs	1	8P-CB

BODYWARE

	Essence Cost	Cost	Availability	Street Index	Legality
Level 2	1.25	40,000¥	3/24 hrs	1.25	6P-CB
Level 3	2.8	90,000¥	3/24 hrs	1.5	5P-CB
Dermal Plating					
Level 1	.5	6,000¥	4/12 days	1	6P-CA
Level 2	1	15,000¥	4/12 days	1	6P-CA
Level 3	1.5	45,000¥	4/12 days	1	5P-CA
Dermal Sheath					
Level 1	.7	24,000¥	6/14 days	1.5	6P-CA
Level 2	1.4	60,000¥	6/14 days	1.5	6P-CA
Level 3	2.1	120,000¥	8/14 days	1.5	5P-CA
Coloration Adaptation	—	+50%	+2/+4 days	+.25	Legal
Cyber Controller	.1	32,000¥	8/14 days	1.5	6P-CA
Filtration Systems					
Air	Rating ÷ 10	Rating x 15,000¥	6/4 days	1	Legal
Blood	Rating ÷ 5	Rating x 10,000¥	6/4 days	1	Legal
Ingested Toxin	Rating ÷ 5	Rating x 10,000¥	6/4 days	1	Legal
Skill Hardwires					
Level 1–4	Level x .2	Level x 5,000¥	6/10 days	1	Legal
Level 5–8	Level x .25	Level x 50,000¥	12/14 days	1.5	6P-CB
Level 9–10	Level x .3	Level x 500,000¥	12/14 days	1.5	4P-CB
Skillwires					
Rating 1–3	.1 x Rating	Rating x 10,000¥	4/10 days	1	Legal
Rating 4–6	.2 x Rating	Rating x 100,000¥	5/10 days	1	6P-CB
Rating 7–9	.3 x Rating	Rating x 1,000,000¥	12/20 days	1	4P-CB
Skillwire Plus					
Level 1–3	Level x .1	Level x 15,000¥	4/10 days	1	Legal
Level 4–6	Level x .2	Level x 125,000¥	5/10 days	1	6P-CB
Level 7–9	Level x .3	Level x 1,000,000 ¥	12/20 days	1	4P-CB
Vehicle Control Rig					
Level 1	2	12,000¥	6/48 hrs	1	6P-CA
Level 2	3	60,000¥	8/48 hrs	1.25	6P-CA
Level 3	5	300,000¥	8/48 hrs	1.5	5P-CA
Wired Reflex Systems					
Standard Wired Reflexes					
Level 1	2	55,000¥	4/8 days	1	5P-CB
Level 2	3	165,000¥	4/8 days	1	4P-CB
Level 3	5	500,000¥	8/14 days	1	3-CC
Reaction Enhancer	.3/point	60,000¥	6/7 days	2	6P-CC
Reflex Trigger	+.2	+13,000¥	As wired reflexes	As wired reflexes	4P-CB
Weapon Mounts					
Articulate Arm	.25	110,000¥	12/24 days	2	2P-CC
External Mount	—	3,200¥	6/4 days	2	3P-CC
Tracking Mount	—	24,000¥	8/7 days	2	3P-CC

Skillsofts

	Concealability	Base Price	Availability	Street Index	Legality
Activesoft	24	Mp x 100¥	6/4 days	1.25	Legal
Datasoft	24	Mp x 100¥*	4/4 days	1.25	Legal
Knowsoft	24	Mp x 150¥	5/4 days	1.25	Legal
Linguasoft	24	Mp x 50¥	6/36 hrs	1.25	Legal

*More valuable data will cost more.

INDEX

BERGTING

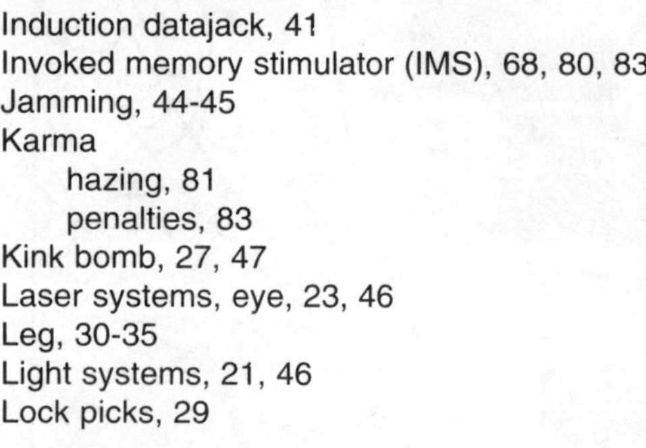
CYBER ARM PROTOYPE
#203P-UI789 12J

You think the *Sixth World* is fragged?

What's the most ugly and malignant creature you can think of?
A toxic spirit? A hoop-kissing suit?

You obviously haven't met the Enemy.

Harlequin thought he beat the Enemy back at the bridge and again in Maui. But his old friend Aina is still being pursued by her own horrible Enemy—even after 7000 years. Their fellow immortal elves might have enough power to defeat this ancient evil... but Aina and Harlequin must convince them to join the battle before it's too late!

WORLDS WITHOUT END

A new Shadowrun® novel by Caroline Spector

Coming in September 1995!

Shadowrun® is a Registered Trademark of FASA Corporation. Copyright © 1995 FASA Corporation. All Rights Reserved.

LOOKS LIKE THIS IS THE END...